TRUMP
and the
Americas

Trump and the Americas

Myriam Witcher

Juan F. Benemelis

2018

BENYA PUBLISHERS

Trump and the Americas
© Copyright 2018
Myriam Witcher
Juan F. Benemelis

Benya Publishers
First Edition.
Printed in U.S.A.

INDEX

The Authors

Myriam Witcher, PhD in economics and finance, businesswoman, journalist and writer, is based in Las Vegas, Nevada.

Myriam is originally from Colombia, she grew up in Bogota the capital. Daughter of a teacher and a doctor who practiced in the former Great Colombian Merchant Fleet.

There she was able to know and enjoy the many facets of a country rich in cultures, human talent, climates and biodiversity. She was also saddened by the evidence of the consequences of violence and the lack of capacity for harmonious resolution of conflicts.

She graduated in economics from the University of Los Andes; then went to study at the University of Hawaii, where she obtained the master in finance and worked as a professor. Later, she obtained the PhD in Finance and Statistics at the famous French University of La Sorbonne, where she was considered an eminent student.

In the United States, she did research at MIT University, while co-authoring the 1,500-page Encyclopedia of Colombia, published in English.

The brilliant economist with a clear vision of the immense wealth of that country, dedicated herself to the business world as a successful entrepreneur, promoting and trading Colombian coffee and flowers on five continents. In these fields, Donald John Trump's books and lectures were one of her instruments of guidance.

From early age, she had a dream: living in the land of the freedom, in the United States. Her father, as doctor of the Colombian fleet, met in New York to Donald Trump, his family and his political thought reading his books, magazines, videos and talks. From there arose her admiration for Trump. After obtaining citizenship of the United States, she married an American Texan.

The loyal Republican woman, of the Hispanic origin, devoted to the Donald Trump campaign of making America great again, since June 2015, when Trump announced his candidature.

In the middle of the presidential campaign, Myriam wrote a book *Donald Trump: America First and Great Again*, which in 2016 was published in English, Spanish and Arabic and is now on Amazon.com.

Immediately, she became a symbol and the new policy that Trump presented; and outside the USA, both in Colombia, Mexico, Spain and so on, Myriam was the enlightenment of the ideas of Donald Trump. Also, as a representative of Trump's campaign, she traveled to the Middle East.

With her colossal journalist activity in radio, internet, and personal not only prevented in the Hispanic community of the whole country, the winning of the other Republican contenders of the primaries in favor of Trump, but also, singlehanded determined the increase of Latin votes in the presidential election.

All US and mainland Hispanic radio stations interviewed her as the spokeswoman for Trump's campaign for the Republican nomination and the presidency.

For the Hispanic, Myriam Witcher was and is not only the personification of the new era that inaugurates Donald Trump, but in his political imaginary considered the Trump-Witcher duo as an inseparable symbol.

Myriam is a unique phenomenon, is today a legend not only with US Hispanics, but in countries throughout the continent, as a symbol of the new era that opens with the presidency of Trump, and a hope to solve the problems that afflict the Hispanic continent.

Myriam combines her ancestral Hispanic culture with the Anglo-Saxon culture, which makes her a profound knower of the problems of the continent and Colombia. Her love and defense of the USA and her denunciation of communism in the continent has led her to fight for the dignity of the Hispanic, to erase the negative image, especially of women, prostitutes, and men, to be drug traffickers or terrorists Guerrillas

She has in-depth knowledge in the field of business, deep in finance and a broad political culture; disciplined with a direct character is also very loyal to her political convictions and support to the current administration and strives to have clear goals, work to achieve them and obtain results.

After the American political campaign, Myriam continues to practice journalism for her love of the USA and her loyalty to President Trump, because she also deeply loves the activity of connecting with the public and serving humanity.

Her intelligence and spirituality has led her to be generous, to give herself to projects in social networks, to contribute to the care of people suffering from cancer, to seek the well-being of orphans and those homeless and to spread the culture of the protection of animals.

Among her hobbies is reading and her favorite sports are swimming and tennis. Today she does it by supporting Donald Trump because she believes that his political project offers the best option for the United States and the world: that is the essence of her previous book *America First and Great Again*, and her co-author of this new book with Juan F. Benemelis.

Juan F. Benemelis. He was born in Cuba, 1942. He lives in the United States.

Graduate in Business Administration in Havana Business University, master in International Law, and PhD in History both from Havana University.

He was a diplomat in Africa and extensively operated in Africa and the Middle East. He served as advisor to Yemen president Salem Robaya Ali in 1976-1978. During the 1980s and early 1990s he was a foreign policy consultant in Washington.

He is an award-winning historian and a published author of more than 50 books and hundreds of essays concerning politics, terrorism, espionage, history, philosophy, physics and so on.

Among his masterpieces is an extensive history of Africa, a profound study of the Quran and the Islamic philosophy, a deep essay about the roots of Islamic terrorism and an extensive study of all the 33 transitions that took place in the former Soviet Bloc.

Benemelis, also known as the Spanish language Kissinger, is considered the foremost expert in Islamic culture, Africa, international politics and terrorism.

He is also a refined poet, a profound mathematician and physicist, and an excellent painter with ongoing exhibitions. A very real and rare renaissance personality.

Many critics have argued that Benemelis is the most prolific and encyclopedic author at least in the Hispanic culture, not only because of the breadth of his work spanning diverse disciplines or the depth of his analysis of the global context of our time, but also by his philosophical views on the human and civilization.

A constant inquirer about the uncertainties and existential crisis that impinges on the economic, social and spiritual work of the contemporary human.

By Way of Introduction
By Myriam Witcher

What has moved to write this book with Dr. Juan F. Benemelis, the most important philosopher and thinker in Latin America, with more than 50 books and at the same time a great painter, has been our great friendship, love and admiration and respect we feel for our American country, and the deep support we have given to our President Donald J. Trump, in the primaries & presidential, and now as President of the United States of America.

Both Dr. Benemelis and I were very active on Facebook, Twitter, political rallies, radio shows and television interviews and directly participating in campaign rallies.

This book is the result of our extensive talks since President Trump announced his aspiration for the presidency. The profound political knowledge of the continent of Benemelis and my long experience in Hispanic countries were combined to offer this contribution to the new administration, of the current political map and the fundamental characteristics of this continent.

Above all, knowing the serious errors and traditional ignorance of USA diplomacy towards the peoples of the southern Rio Grande, something that has worsened in recent decades.

Our native countries, Cuba and Colombia, have suffered 60 years of struggle and pain; To witness injustice, loss of life, lack of freedom of expression, in which the middle class, the vital force that sustains these Hispanic countries, every day goes to the abyss without having a relief or a solution.

Castro Communist Cuba has penetrated the entire continent as a Hydra, inoculating hatred for the USA, promoting left-wing ideologies, guerrillas, violence, terrorism, protecting narco-trafficking and currently controlling countries like Venezuela, Nicaragua, Ecuador, Bolivia and the danger that Colombia will be next.

The disappearance of Castro's communism in Cuba would mean a total reversal for the whole continent, which could then rebuild the democratic road that was interrupted precisely by Havana. This has been very difficult to understand by the American presidents on duty, although we are convinced that it will not be with the current Donald Trump.

The double standards of the political elite in many Latin American countries make freedom and prosperity far from democracy and peace. The collapse of the democratic system in Cuba and Venezuela, and the danger of the same happening in Colombia, has altered the continent's geo-politics against the United States.

The peoples of Cuba, Colombia, Venezuela, Nicaragua, Ecuador and Bolivia deserve "Peace and Freedom". That is why the true democracies of the continent, with the United States in the lead, must defend all citizens of democratic societies in the Hispanic countries that must live in peace and freedom.

Colombians know that the current "long civil war", violence, corruption and narco-terrorism are not solved by the current Cuban engineered peace process. Communist Cuba, Venezuela and Colombia have sunk in narco-terrorism and in the production and marketing of cocaine and opium into the United States and Europe.

USA has a new beginning, a new era, a new approach to improving the life of the entire American continent, guaranteeing the democratic feeling that makes us the same that makes us American citizens above all, our original New World, our individual interests, to think as a single entity with its diversities, and to take this opportunity with a president with deep sincerity to think about our land, to defend our beliefs, our economy, our life.

Both Dr. Benemelis and I are convinced that President Trump will also fight for the whole continent, to establish social justice, family values, to banish vices, illegalities, to make streets, our spaces, places safe for our children, without fear of drugs, violence, corrupt ideologies.

Since 9/11/01, the sense of security across the continent has changed. National Security must be the priority for the entire American continent. In addition to other alliances in the world, Central America, South America and the Caribbean Basin should be the main strategic partners of the United States. We are a

Continent-Island protected by two oceans; our geography dictates our geo-politics, a concept missing by the traditional USA diplomacy.

We must stop the entry into our countries of terrorists, a clear protection at the borders. We have high levels of unemployment on the continent, illegal immigrants, terrorists and illicit drugs; debt and the fiscal deficit is a chronic evil of all their economies; crime and overcrowding in prisons are evils that await a solution.

We need a change of direction where constitutions are respected, where presidents cease to govern over legislatures and legal bodies. The current health care system is a real disaster; education is influenced by a whole ideology and partisan of the extreme left, where abused anti-American texts abound.

United States should transform its contribution into an expression of hope, recognition, gratitude and love for the Latin American people towards the American people and the US President.

Based on programs of productive transformation several strategic sectors of the economy should be selected to transform the industry and promote the development of companies in the whole continent, investing in transportation networks, railroads, canals, air transportation infrastructure, energy and water infrastructure, telecommunications infrastructure and the agro-industrial sector.

With the intervention of God and President Trump, democracy can be restored throughout the continent, and clean elections, such as those held in the United States that presided over Donald Trump, can finally take place.

The United States under the Trump administration will become "Great Again", although it can be much more so if the entire American continent, from the Great Lakes to Patagonia, manages to be "Much Great." America does not end in the Rio Grande, America comprises of the North Pole to the South Pole, with the corsage of Caribbean islands.

And as Dr. Benemelis says constantly, USA security and greatness are inextricably linked to the rest of the American continent, much more so than to Europe or Asia, something that, while well understood by the presidents of the XIX century, from George Washington to Theodore "Teddy" Roosevelt, however, throughout the 20th century was ignored by the following presidents of this nation.

President Donald Trump responds categorically to the question "Power for what? One of the axes on which the new American political guidelines are built with his intelligent and creative thinking: continue to fight against narco-traffic-terrorism and make America Great Again. We can add that in the hands of President Trump is also the fate of the whole continent, the dream and conviction of the Founding Fathers of this nation, to make the continent "Great, Great, Greater than ever."

Let us hope that this book can be read and not remain as one more on the shelves of libraries. God Bless all our readers, God Bless America, God Bless President Trump.

Foreword by
Juan F. Benemelis

In the North American political arena and in the academic circles, there are those that minimize the importance of the region within US foreign policy and, on the other hand, those (a few) who maintain that it has a first-order value within the strategy of perpetuating the global supremacy of the United States.

Added to this is the inability shown by the US political system during the post-bipolar period to reach a consensus on foreign policy with a degree of consistency similar to that achieved after World War II.

The level of activity of US foreign policy in each moment and region of the world is related, above all, to the degree to which its strategic interests are being effectively challenged by other actors in each geographical area.

It is therefore natural that regions such as East Asia, the Middle East and Eastern Europe, scenarios of increasing competitiveness among the great powers, demand a level of activity - expressed particularly in terms of military and diplomatic presence- much greater than that dedicated to other regions of the world perceived as relatively safe.

From the undue identification of what is important and what is a priority, it is often the case that, to measure the importance assigned by the USA to Latin America and the Caribbean, only visits to the highest level of the US government of (or, rather, the lack of them and widespread ignorance about the region demonstrated again and again by its highest authorities) as evidence to argue that USA "forget" or "neglect" Latin America and the Caribbean.

Is notable the scarcity (or even complete absence) of references to Latin America and the Caribbean in the strategic documents and in the speeches of the American presidents. Also, the academic analysts also pay little attention to it.

After focusing its attention on Afghanistan, Iraq and Syria, the USA has subordinated its consideration to Latin America and, to a certain extent, neglecting its hegemonic vocation on the continent, which has suffered a long period of distancing and geopolitical lethargy.

The vast area of Latin America has more natural resources than any other area on the planet, to become an economic giant on a par with the United States, much more than Europe, Russia, India or China.

USA had devoted more attention and development effort to Europe, China or India, but having dedicated instead such efforts to Latin America and the Caribbean, in geo-political, economic, technical and investment's terms, the region were now the world's second largest economic powerhouse, with the advantage to be much more politically integrated to the USA and to be unconditional strategic ally.

But the USA never thought of such long-term geo-strategic terms. However, he still has time to do so, especially because doing such a project would prevent China, for example, from becoming an economic giant on a par with the USA.

At present, the United States lacks a strategic vision of the region, which is still absent from the agenda of Washington politicians, who live disconnected from the new reality of the region, and only interested in electoral periods, in search of Hispanic vote.

It may be that Latin America is not pondered at this precise moment as a matter of great strategic importance, or short-term priority, because it is erroneously considered an insured region that does not require greater attention or allocation of resources.

Latin America

The idea of a "Western Hemisphere" according to which the countries of Latin America and the United States would be united among themselves and would be distinguished from the rest of the world by common interests, values, perceptions and policies, no longer adjusts to reality, both from the Washington's point of view as from Buenos Aires, Santiago, Sao Paulo or Brasilia.

Latin America is not a unit, and less so in relation to the relationship with the United States, despite representing the region a very important market for North American trade.

Therefore, to understand inter-American relations it is necessary to distinguish, at least, four different regions: a) Mexico, Central America and the Caribbean islands; b) Brazil c) Argentina and the rest of the Mercosur countries, e) and the Andean countries that require further disaggregation.

Mexico, Central America and the Caribbean, is the most integrated area to the United States, and represent about 50% of US investments, 70% of interregional trade and from there comes 85% of migrants to the USA.

The countries of the region differ enormously from each other. Argentina is so different from Haiti, or Peru from Panama, or the Dominican Republic from Chile, as Sweden is from Turkey, or Australia from Indonesia. Is that, although in the last thirty years almost all Latin American countries have agreed to adopt democratic elections and built market economies that respect the macroeconomic equilibrium, some key differences have been increased.

During the last decade, Latin America has become a region of middle-income countries, with growth faster than the global average and a reduction in trade deficits, thanks to a rise in commodity prices, the improvement of investments and the growth of internal markets.

At the same time the potential economic value of the region has increased as an attractive market for the products of the industrialized countries and to receive capital.

With $ 700 billion of monetary reserves, 400 million inhabitants, large reserves of hydrocarbons, energy autonomy, important mining deposits, the greatest biodiversity on the planet, it has the necessary elements to build a scheme of autonomy in the geostrategic area.

Latin America and the Caribbean, with 12% of the total land area and 6% of the world population, own 27% of the planet's fresh water. Their water reserves become a vital strategic control factor for a not too distant future. Hence the importance of the Guaraní Aquifer, in the triple Argentine-Brazilian-Paraguayan border also including Uruguay, is a fabulous freshwater reserve.

35% of the hydro-energetic power, 27% of the coal, enough for three centuries of exploitation. 24% of the oil, 8% of the gas and

5% of the uranium are in this region. Venezuela, for example, stores 300 billion barrels of oil in its subsoil, enough for 4 centuries of production at the current rate,

To which must be added 40% of the world's biodiversity and 25% of the forest cover of the whole world, as well as important strategic mineral deposits (bauxite, coltan, niobium, thorium), besides iron, fundamental for the technologies of tip (including military)

The region of Latin America and the Caribbean, one of the geographic areas closest to the equator, is one of the most abundant in biodiversity, a wealth that is found mainly in tropical humid forests and Coral reefs.

According to the FAO, the region contains 40% of the planet's plant and animal species and is considered to have the highest floristic diversity in the world.

The Amazon valleys, the cold Andean mountains, the Brazilian Atlantic forest and the dry forests of Mesoamerica are home to some of the richest ecosystems in the world. Brazil, Paraguay and Bolivia share some of the most important continental wetlands in the world, including 400,000 square kilometers of marshes.

Around 25% of all those resources that the United States consumes come from the Latin American subcontinent. The wide wealth of natural resources guarantees the ability to invest in the construction of an alternative technological-industrial development model, in accordance with the new environmental sustainability agendas.

The growth of advertising spending in Latin America is faster than in the rest of the world. In 2016 it is estimated that it spent 31 trillion in the region only on the internet, compared to 17 trillion in 2011. On television it reached 30 trillion dollars in 2016. In printed newspapers, it increased to 10 trillion dollars.

In fact, Latinos are 15% of the US population and represent almost 50% of the total population growth rate.

This energy wealth is much closer geographically to the USA and is safer. Also, the privatization process may lead to the exploration, exploitation and distribution of Latin American and Caribbean energy as much as possible in USA hands.

Latin American fragmentation contributes to the encouragement of related groups, and countries that belong to various organizations, giving rise to new cooperation schemes. This new multilateralism that is being built, is going through a transition in which institutionality constitutes a contradiction, but also a great challenge.

With the accession of many Latin American countries to the WTO, trade between both areas was gradually liberalized. If we add to this the progressive development of a middle class with a certain purchasing power, the penetration of North American products in the Latin American market is increasing.

Within a tendency to conform regions and sub-regions, groups such as UNASUR, ALBA, CELAC and the Pacific Alliance can be listed. Some of them, such as ALBA and UNASUR, are under the leadership of Venezuela and Brazil and with a defensive multilateralism. Others, such as the Pacific Alliance, present a cooperative multilateralism and shared leadership.

US exports to Latin America and the Caribbean have declined over the past decade, and China has been filling that gap, while India's trade with the region also grows considerably. The United States has become Brazil's second trading partner, after China. The bilateral trade between both countries reached 100 billion dollars, but there is no reason why that number does not reach 400 or 500 billion.

Latin America shows a growing interest in Asian countries, and in turn China, India, Korea and Japan have been increasing their presence in Latin America doing a counterweight to the traditional US hegemony. Hence the fear of the United States and its interest in re-approaching Latin America. And the Pacific Alliance could be the means and the spearhead for that rearrangement.

We are witnessing a new multilateral architecture and regional governance, responding to the lack of interest of the United States in Latin America, changes at the regional and international level and the search for a new multilateralism with the participation of non-governmental actors.

With a GDP equivalent to US\$ 6 trillion, Latin America and the Caribbean should be the last region of the world to be lost by the United States in terms of its permanent or "vital" interests, to keep it out of reach and excessive influence of other extra continental powers.

The countries of Latin America and the Caribbean, for their part, will continue to arouse Washington's concern, since they constitute significant markets, important sources of investment and fundamental sources of raw materials and migrants. They are, in addition, test fields for democratic governance and the market economy, as well as active participants in the international community.

One Continent

Indeed, it can be said that the political and economic connection with the American continent has been the most lasting and constant feature of US foreign policy since its very emergence.

Throughout the history of the United States, certain events on this continent suddenly acquired the highest attention of the leaders and a greater allocation of resources in foreign policy, such as "Teddy· Roosevelt's Latin American policy, or the John F. Kennedy Crisis of Atomic Missiles, the Falkland Islands crisis, or the current situation in Venezuela.

North America was colonized by British settlers, who brought with them the structure of property rights and the 1st Industrial Revolution. In a context of relative political and economic freedom with institutions, the result was the gradual evolution of a free society in the decades that followed independence.

The independence of the United States was a great example for the countries of the region, especially the Bill of Rights of Virginia. Although the Latin American independences would have a different outcome.

In 1823, US President James Monroe enunciated the phrase "America for the Americans" who was the so-called Monroe Doctrine and Pan Americanism, which established that European states had no right to intervene in American affairs.

President Alexander Hamilton predicted the creation of a great American system, which would not subject itself to the control and influence of any force beyond the Atlantic, and the United States Congress after 1880 devoted much attention to Latin America, as never before.

It is true that the United States championed many independences, mainly in Central America, whether with political, economic or military support, but its great influence would begin with the Monroe Doctrine.

Although the Latin American independences followed the constitutional example of the United States, the results were dissimilar. Iberian colonialism generated political instability and economic monopolies that still persist today, with adverse consequences for a dynamic economic growth.

The reason for their historical and current delays with respect to the US, was that they failed to obtain stable parliamentary regimes, nor were the constitutional precepts respected nor did they regard the independent judicial bodies that guaranteed the fulfillment of the contracts.

Without a legacy of relatively free governments, the region staged half a century of territorial or political wars, coups and dictatorships, which tried to fill the gap left by the Iberian governments (Spain and Portugal),

It is in this context that the Monroe Doctrine (1823) signified a backing for the Latin American independence processes, with the declaration: "America for the Americans".

The Latin American countries, inheritors of an elitist and unstable colonial social structure, created more space between the growing power of the United States and the increasingly weak Latin American countries, with their deplorable internal socioeconomic conditions, corrupt political and economic elites and oligarchic and the distance between a commercial urban world and an overwhelming and abandoned rural society.

By 1880, the United States reached industrial production in Great Britain and in the following decade surpassed it (Davis 07). Given this scenario is that James Blaine seeks to strengthen ties and commercial ties with Latin America to leave out the European powers. In this panorama takes place the first meeting of American nations in Washington known as Pan-Americanism.

In the 19th century, North American investments created a huge agro-mining market. Later, in the 20th century, with the export of industrial technology, North American capital consolidated the national bourgeoisies and the working class.

At the beginning of the 20th century, the United States created directly the democratic nations of Cuba, Panama and Nicaragua.

Both Admiral Alfred T. Mahan and President "Teddy" Roosevelt based their ideas on the

Monroe Doctrine. Mahan unites for the first time the concept of "national interest" with Ibero-America over ideologies proclaiming to export the political model in what he considered as "our natural continent", especially the closest territories, to preserve them from harmful and outdated interference (Mahan 1890).

The evolution of two regions so united and at the same time so separate, since the Pan-Americanism of 1889, the TIAR of 1945 and the Organization of American States in 1948 was marked with successes and failures, but based on the concept of "America for the Americans", as evidenced from its beginning.

In the future, the ideology, culture and foreign policy of the United States, accompanied by an economic machinery, was carried out in response to a civilizing mission.

The projection of the United States towards Latin America and the Caribbean, from the proclamation of the Monroe Doctrine to the present day, has been marked by an impregnable line of continuity, consisting in relying on our region to strengthen its position within of the correlation of forces between the great powers and, in the conditions after World War II, to develop a strategy of hegemony on a world scale.

The Pan-American meeting of Panama in 1939, promoted by the USA, showed how carefully Washington handled the situation in continental America. There was adopted a resolution to remove from the Americas the propaganda of doctrines that "put in danger the common American democratic ideal".

Diplomacy, together with the American military apparatus, undertake the task of constructing what is initially described as an inter-American system for intercontinental defense against possible aggressions by the Nazi-fascist axis.

The Latin American ruling elites were absolutely favorable to the US, especially after the failure of the League of Nations, which led to a redefinition of relations among the American States. The postwar period in the Continent was marked by the Cold War, the Argentine Peronism, the Castro-communist revolution, the Missiles Crisis, the guerrilla warfare, etc.

In the decades of the 60s and 70s, Latin America was an important fact for the United States. The strategy was based on three objectives: a security imperative to block extra-hemispheric powers; ideological objectives to counter the Soviet Union and communism and encourage capitalist development.

Thus, the Inter-American Treaty of Reciprocal Assistance is proposed in Mexico; the Pan American Union is transformed into the Organization of American States (OAS), which crystallizes a Latin America more economically and psychologically integrated to the United States.

In a report presented by strategist George F. Kennan after a trip to Latin America in February and March 1950, he pointed out the military importance of the countries of Latin America (Kennan 51). In Rio de Janeiro the continental defense treaty is articulated, the first one of the Cold War, conforming a politico-military block with the United States.

In 1954, USA was forced on National Security grounds to promote armed opposition in Guatemala, against internal subversion and attempts to establish a communist regime in that country. Thus, we have the case in the Dominican Republic, when in 1965 intervened with more than 42,000 soldiers,

Brazil's collaboration for the US occupation of the Dominican Republic illustrates this model, as well as Argentina's support for Reagan administration interventions in Central America in the early 1980s.

In previous decades, the Alliance for Progress, the Initiative for the Americas fulfilled that function and there is currently no such vision. With the Condor Plan, the United States developed many Latin American armies and served to aid governments in the continent that prevented the intrusion of communism and defend the interests of the United States.

During these years, the United States developed a vast plan of aid for development through the Agency for International Development (AID). To this were added sugar quotas, preferential tariffs and other forms of stimulation of economic growth, in addition to the active diplomacy of the State Department, funding and advice to political parties, and the work of the Information Agency (USIA).

From the 1980s, after the collapse of Vietnam, the United States based its strengthening as a continental partnership on the notion of progress. Since the 1990s, democracy had stabilized in the region, expanding market economies and future prospects.

Especially after the dismantling of Castro's design in Granada in 1983; the financing and logistics of the Nicaraguan anti-communist struggle between 1982 and 1987, and the invasion of Panama, dictatorial regimes had fallen and a path towards democracy and equal rights was pursued that would continue even in the 90s.

The large multinationals would settle in Latin America, many companies would expand in the region, governments would sign important agreements with the United States, it seemed that the difficult moments had ended and that the continental alliance would mean a rapid insertion in the world and in the world economy.

Quickly, Argentina, Brazil, Chile, Colombia, Mexico and many Central American countries would strengthen ties with the United States, bringing economic benefits and political support. What country in Latin America did not seek in the 90s the friendship of the United States to benefit economically and have a better image worldwide?

What is significant about these agreements is that Washington did not have to make any concessions in its agricultural export sector nor did it reduce its import quotas to more than 200 products. On the other hand, it gained access to the financial, service, high technology, health, education and media sectors of its counterparts.

Organizations such as USAID and the NED were dedicated to strengthening and coordinating the elites of each country. Also began a process in which the US dollar replaced national currencies producing stability to Latin American economies, guided by the US Federal Reserve.

However, the United States squandered this situation and changed its continental policy after the disappearance of the Soviet bloc, when the priority became the fight against terrorism, drugs and immigration.

Then, the political and economic instability became generalized and the Castro-communist design took advantage promoting the statist and building a political and economic block against the United States, at the same time as the cultivation and production of drugs intensified in countries like Mexico, Colombia, Peru and Bolivia.

The Santa Fe IV Document, the Strategic Document for the year 2020 of the United States Army and the report Global Trends 2015, of the National Intelligence Council, present the hypothesis of social conflict only from the perspective of a military struggle.

While the US strategy was organized from the geopolitical school of Nicholas Spykman, evident in the actions in Eurasia, Spykman himself warned that the true "perimeter of security" and last line of defense of the United States global hegemony was Latin America that should become a zone of contention for extra continental rivals through a Pan-American continental market and defense agreements (Fiori 07).

Although the United States has some 70 military bases with high technology that complement the Fourth Naval Fleet, it would draw attention to its "unconcern" for the proliferation of pro-communist regimes. The Mérida Initiative, signed in 2008 between Presidents George Bush and Felipe Calderón, involved military training in Mexico, the sale of weapons and the control of the overflight of unmanned spy planes. A year later, the USA-Colombia military agreement was signed.

The United States promised to support and strengthen the entire region, but the Bush and William J. Clinton administrations focused on the Middle East.

In the 1960s, it would have been difficult to imagine Washington accepting political leaders such as Daniel Ortega in Nicaragua, Hugo Chavez and Nicolás Maduro in Venezuela, Evo Morales in Bolivia, Luiz Inácio Lula da Silva in Brazil, Ricardo Lagos and Michelle Bachelet in Chile, Tabaré Vázquez in Uruguay, Leonel Fernández in the Dominican Republic.

All this not only undermined the Pan American solidarity with the United States and its political influence to deal with most of the continental and international crises, but also made it lose its economic advantages in the region. It is no longer the main commodity market in Latin America, nor the great exporter of machinery and technology. As a consequence, it had lost its political influence.

At that time, organizations such as the Community of Latin American and Caribbean States (Celac), the Union of South American Nations (Unasur), a revival of the Common Market of the South (Mercosur) and the Castro-Chavez design of ALBA appeared.

Then Secretary of State Colin Powell became aware of USA's power and influence crisis in the continent and in 2002 he tried to launch a Free Trade Area of the Americas, the FTAA, to guarantee US companies control from the territory that goes from the Arctic to the Antarctic and the free access without obstacle or difficulty to our products, services, technology and capital throughout the hemisphere.

The scenario of Sino-American and Russian-American inter-hegemonic rivalry in Latin America, promoted and managed by Castro-communism, must redefine sub-regional and continental security initiatives.

Geostrategy in Latin America

What about Latin America? What about that region so close to the world superpower? What was its relationship with the continent as the historical processes were carried out? Is the region still the so-called "Backyard" of the most important country in the world or is there a much stronger and rooted relationship?

It could be argued that Latin America, in contrast to what is being propagated, is in fact the most important strategic area for the United States; that it does not receive the resources it judges to deserve, that it does not receive the strategic treatment, is another matter.

The strategic significance of Latin America and the Caribbean during the historic evolutionary process of the United States, from an incipient independent republic to the acquisition of its present status as the world's first and only superpower, is unobjectionable.

The relations between Latin America and the US are in a phase of very rapid changes. Unlike the relations between the two regions that marked much of the nineteenth and twentieth centuries, everything indicates that what will characterize the present century will have a different sign.

We start from a supposed western hemisphere with shared values, or from the reading that frames them in a practice influenced by the thesis of the loss of importance of Latin America for the USA.

Because of the political changes in the governments of the region, the United States no longer has the political unconditionality of the Cold War era, today there are more distant governments and seeking greater autonomy in their relations, due to the diversity of positions much more marked in recent years.

This makes it relatively easy to influence policies linked to issues that do not involve central security matters. But, at the same time, it becomes very difficult to coordinate or control such policies, something that is not and will not be very frequent, given the amount of other questions and relationships that the US has to handle.

On the main political issues, Washington and the region disagree. In these types of subjects that encompass topics such as international trade and the effort to build a new financial architecture there are no great coincidences. In matters of political framework, such as the role of Cuba and Venezuela in the hemisphere, or the problematic subject of illegal immigration, there are no points of agreement either.

It is difficult to exaggerate the number of concerns that compete with Latin America for the attention of policymakers in the US. Not only the special circumstances of Iraq and Syria, the dilemma of Israel and the ghosts of a nuclear Iran or a North Korea detract from the importance of the region. Latin America rarely shines at the center of the North American radar.

Any international organization is, in a way, more important than the Organization of American States (OAS). Therefore, it is ironic that the system of inter-American presidential summits has flourished at a time when regional policies have less and less meaning.

The crucial policies for the future of the region are routinely established outside of Latin America, and the impact they produce is usually more residual than intentional. Latin American countries are highly vulnerable to trends, events and exogenous decisions and rarely exercise significant influence in matters outside the region,

The North American policies that affect Latin America and the Caribbean are determined not only by international power relations and external challenges, but also by the interaction between the influences of different regions, sectors and internal groups.

In the United States it is not clear that there is total coherence in its foreign policy, some are the priorities of the Southern Command -with great weight in certain regional countries and a look at security key- and others of the State Department, not to mention the of agencies like the DEA, or those of the North American Congress in the field of international relations.

The Department of State, the Pentagon and the CIA are no longer the only - or the main - government agencies relevant to the region, as they were between the 1950s and the 1980s. For many countries in Latin America, the Secretary of the Treasury, The President of the Federal Reserve and the Secretary of Commerce are as important as the Secretary of State.

The governors of California, Texas and Florida are significant for certain issues and countries. They also impact the American Anti-Drug Agency (DEA), the Department of Agriculture and the Federal Judicial Branch. Business matters such as pharmaceuticals, computers, immigration lobbies are important. So also, the problems raised by criminal organizations, including the drug cartels, and the police, et cetera.

For Latin American countries, the problems of the US Congress are as important as the executive power, being more open to social influences and impulses. As a result, the development of policies towards the United States is a huge and permanent challenge for any country in the region.

Historically, Latin America had for the United States a status of temporary partners, with all the consequences of instability that this implies for the region. Paradoxically, the linear visions of long-term trends in the exercise of US power in Latin America have little vision of the future and have proven to be wrong repeatedly over more than 50 years. Even a cursory glance at the dramatic changes of power in the past provides ample evidence that changes in power can be abrupt and profound.

For global politics, the most important living space is Eurasia, which implies the so-called "Latin American irrelevance" thesis, according to which this does not represent a priority in the US foreign policy agenda. Thus, in these first decades of the 21st century, the logic of "close distance" and "selective bilateralism" prevails.

The policy actions directed to the countries of the Southern Hemisphere, in general, are oriented to cover short-term needs or to be coordinated with the strategies directed to the area of priority interests. Other cases of the logic of US priorities that damaged the continental concert were the United States' support for England in the Malvinas Islands conflict against Argentina, proving that it was an ally without strategic relevance.

Towards the end of the Cold War, geopolitics and military technologies changed and the importance of the Panama Canal declined. This alteration implied an overturn of the continent in which many countries turned to the left and populism, under the influence of Castro-communism and its affiliate Venezuelan President Hugo Chávez.

This was also evidenced by the election of the Chilean Insulza as Secretary General of the OAS, and the fact that for the first time in history, the United States did not achieve support for its candidate. What do you think about the unattached project of a channel in Nicaragua, which also has serious environmental, political, ethnic and social consequences?

How was it possible that traditional partners, Mercosur and others in the Continent, from the OAS and based on articles 15, 19 21 of the OAS Charter, expressed their disagreement with the events of the guerrilla in Ecuador.

But relations between the countries of the Western Hemisphere can no longer be captured in general phrases or simple paradigms: inter-American relations will continue to be determined by global challenges and opportunities, by domestic pressures and demands, both from the US and Latin America, and for regional and sub-regional developments.

Today, the agendas are much more specific and local. The contemporary concerns of the US in relation to Latin America refer basically to practical issues of trade, finance, energy and other resources, as well as to the management of shared problems that cannot be solved individually by each country: the fight against terrorism, the battle against drug and arms trafficking, protection of public health and the environment, energy stability and migration control.

Washington should no longer deploy a single "Latin American policy," but different bilateral or sub-regional strategies: Mexico, Central America and the Caribbean make up a deeply integrated area, through migration and trade, to the United States.

In general, the US agenda for Latin America must recover a geopolitical vision, national security and democratic ideology, to interpose leftist populism and Castro-communism. Not only should be focused on the economy, within the framework of shared problems such as drug trafficking, and migration.

US foreign policy towards Latin America needs to look at two fronts. First, in its internal economic, social and cultural processes. Second, its projection to the world forced by its civilizing mission and internal disputes in Latin America.

In the coming years, relationships will remain complex, multifaceted and contradictory. This is not mainly because recent American governments have lacked vision or imagination; what is most scarce, in fact, are substantial bases for significant global policies towards the region.

It is necessary to understand the old geopolitical projects towards Latin America, to create new organizations that portray the complexities and the attempts of the American continent in trying to recover its special relationship with the United States and create regional agreements in political, economic, social and military matters.

The confusion is that the strategic importance of Latin America for the United States is historical, since the very founding of the American nation and for that reason it has a permanent and lasting character, which by definition is not cyclical, such as European or Asian countries.

Despite the war against Islamic terrorism, disagreements with Russia and the dilemma with China, the United States should not neglect its policy with its mainland neighbors; a continent too rich, too near to let in enemy hands.

Latin America Security

US diplomacy has lost weight even in several South American countries, precisely when the current Latin American political moment is very delicate. Even in the electoral area that one of its strengths was appreciated, today there are signs of a lack of deepening.

And what can we say about the levels of continental security in the face of the serious complications that are confronted internationally? In that, the area is behind. It is no longer just a dilemma of guerrillas and bullets. Now there are other elements that are capital for the global and hemispheric economy, such as oil and gas.

USA does not have a plan that goes beyond the fight against drug trafficking, migration issues and a commercial agenda, and because there is a consensus in the region, mainly in Brazil and Argentina, that economies must open.

In addition to counteracting and controlling transnational phenomena that are threatening US democratic society: Castro-communist states, corrupt and clientele's political tradition, drug trafficking, organized crime and migration.

Does the United States have a clear focus to continue building on the achievements made in the past decades, does the United States have the courage to establish and defend the principles favorable to American interests?

If US policymakers rearrange the ingredients of their policy to re-articulate the processes of Latin America and the Caribbean under their jurisdiction, it is because its objectives in that sense are part of its global geostrategic projection.

It is essential in the new political environment to promote a new generation of leaders who are looking for a new direction for Latin America. That would allow the United States to begin again its relationship with its neighbors, especially with some who throughout history have accused Washington of imperialist or negligent, or both.

The United States can achieve the promotion of more able leaders to end the vertiginous process of corruption and robbery of public money to advance democracy, economic progress and social peace.

That is why it is necessary to develop a hemispheric agenda to introduce its priority themes, including the consolidation of democracy and human rights, and to regain its political presence at the continental level. The United States can help make Latin American economies more competitive and stable by promoting investment in technology, innovation and quality education.

During the Cold War, any US policy toward Latin America was subordinated to the global "geopolitical" confrontation with the Soviet Union, with formulas of containment of the enemy.

The changes in US policy at the beginning of the 21st century, the anti-terrorist war and military interventions in Afghanistan and Iraq, the new national security strategy after the September 11, 2001 attacks on US territory, marked a new stage with direct repercussions for the region.

It is erroneous to consider that the national security of the United States is possible by securing only the territory of the American nation. United States national security includes and depends on continental security, the entire territory of continental America and the Caribbean.

In turn, the United States cannot claim to maintain a position of world supremacy if they are not able to do so essentially and exclusively in the Western Hemisphere.

Not only to maintain an overwhelming superiority on the strategic-military plane in the American continent, but also to guarantee access, under advantageous conditions, to the strategic natural resources present in the region.

According to the US SouthCom Strategy Partnership for the Americas, the Latin American and Caribbean nations are strategically important to the national security and economic future of the United States. The long-term interests of the U.S. are best served by a hemisphere of stable, secure with democratic nations. A prosperous future for all rests on a foundation of shared values; efficient governments; free societies; and open, market-based economies.

In military and security matters, the US must increase the total number of Latin American military personnel trained by the Pentagon, and increase treaties to share sensitive information.

US defense policy for the Western Hemisphere should include the OAS and each of the inter-military commitments, promoting a strong system of defense cooperation that addresses the complex challenges of the 21st century.

We must not forget the hand of Castro-communism in the eviction of the SouthCom of Panama in 1999 (Torrijos-Carter agreement), and in the closing of the Manta base in Ecuador, decreed by President Rafael Correa in 2009.

The Task Ahead

USA should avoid the potential geopolitical turbulence that could impact US citizens and military personnel in the region, particularly due to anti-American actions in Cuba, Nicaragua, Bolivia and Venezuela, should be avoided. The purchase of Sino-Russian arms and the growing influence of Iran must be hampered.

The summits of the Defense Ministers of the Americas, as well as the activities of the IADB - described by the Pentagon as "the oldest multilateral military organization in the world" - and of its various dependencies should be promoted. Likewise, the systematic realization of the Conference of American Armies, the Inter-American Naval Conference and the System of Cooperation of the American Air Forces.

Also, training of Latin American and Caribbean military and civilians through various bilateral programs and Pentagon institutions, such as the Center for Hemispheric Defense Studies (HDSC) and the Institute for Cooperation for the Security of the Western Hemisphere, the former "School of the Americas".

In addition, the Pentagon must further promote inter-American military exercises through the SouthCom, which also includes Canadian and NATO military forces that still hold various positions in the insular and continental Caribbean: France, Great Britain and the Netherlands.

The close political, economic and military cooperation of the countries of the region is a strategic issue for the defense of the United States. If we stop giving military attention to the region, we are going to regret SouthCom's lack of advanced bases (FOL).

Regional commanders must be proactive now in setting up new bases. We must take advantage of the case of Argentina ready to reestablish military cooperation suspended since 2009.

Together with Peru, Argentina is vital for the replenishment and betting of its ships of the 4th Southern Command Fleet, which patrols the Atlantic and South Pacific oceans. The Falkland Islands are a strategic point for their projection on Antarctica, South America, South Africa and the South Pacific, South Atlantic and Indian oceans.

Likewise, the North American presence on the South Atlantic, now shared with other extra-regional powers members of NATO and in particular with Great Britain, should be strengthened.

The Brazilian government must agree to share "responsibilities and costs" with the United States in the defense and security of the Western Hemisphere, especially in the South American Defense Council, to help forge interdependence and further integrate the friendly armed forces.

The United States should expand its strategic partnership with Colombia, which embodies a key role for the peace and security of the continent. Colombia is necessary to guarantee control of the Panama Canal; for the works of expansion of the Canal and for the installation of different American military facilities in the Panamanian territory.

Likewise, the Colombian Navy has always cooperated with the United States in controlling the two maritime entrances of the Panama Canal. Among them, it is worth mentioning their cooperation with all the military maneuvers they have deployed and that will deploy the SouthCom and the Fourth Fleet of the US Navy.

Honduras must remain the key country for all Central America, with the Palmerola base where the Joint Task Force Bravo is stationed, with army units, joint security forces and the Air Force battalion-regiment.

Likewise, the military relationship with Paraguay should be deepened, expanding the scholarship program to Paraguayan military personnel, for training and courses in the USA.

The SouthCom must expand the preparation of the South American armies for future combats against terrorism, and the armies of the continent must be modernized as has been done with Chile and Colombia.

The popularity of the United States has been greatly affected, especially during the last stage of its rule, which did not meet the numerous challenges in almost all the Latin American spheres that the "red wave" presented, or the rise of pro-communist governments and of the left with different radicalism.

The presidency of Barack Obama neglected the region, and was too soft with the Venezuelan Castro and dictators, allowing the advance of the so-called "Bolivarian axis."

Months after his oath, at the V Summit of the Americas held in Trinidad and Tobago in April 2009, President Obama asserted that no Latin American country was considered a threat to the United States, deaf to the implementation of the "Castro-communism" of the so-called "Bolivarian axis" of Cuba, Venezuela, Nicaragua, Bolivia, Ecuador and the threat that looms over Colombia.

The Obama administration, like its predecessor since Reagan's presidency, never understood Latin America, to the point of granting unilateral concessions to Cuba and allowing Havana to manipulate the "peace settlement" in Colombia.

Such a mistake was evident in the then Secretary of State John Kerry's address to the OAS in 2013, characterizing both events as "the end of the Monroe Doctrine", while behind the scenes Cuba turned the area into a global game board, promoting the Entry of China and Russia across the continent.

For a failed foreign president, the Cuban case was probably his best option to do something meaningful and favorable that could tax his legacy before the end of the last presidential term and note a success in foreign policy, which contributed to a possible Democratic permanence in the White House because of the elections of 2016.

What will happen about future relations with Colombia, Venezuela and Cuba? Everything indicates that there will be important changes in the relations of these three countries and the USA. Although little was said during the USA presidential campaign of it, there are likely to be turns in USA foreign policy as opposed to the policy pursued by President Obama.

The most serious crisis facing Trump presidency in the Hemisphere, which is that of Venezuela. A less naive position is needed than the one shown by the State Department led by John Kerry, who on four occasions led to various approaches and dialogues with the Nicolas Maduro regime, which continued with its domestic repression and hostility to Washington.

Previously, SouthCom's current chief, Gen. John Kelly, had sued members of the US Senate Armed Services Committee to turn their attention to the current Venezuelan situation, since - in his view - "he is falling apart in front of us and, unless there is a miracle that causes the opposition or the government of Maduro to retreat, is going to rush towards the economic and democratic catastrophe. "

Venezuela had a discreet presence in the USA presidential campaign. In the first place, Maduro's government identified itself with the Democrats' dirty election war, accusing President

Trump of censoring the press, of being repressive and autocratic.

Russia, China and Iran

To this end, Cuban diplomacy introduced Venezuela into Africa, into the Islamic world, into China and into countries antagonistic to the United States like Iran, Syria, Muammar Gaddafi's Libya, North Korea, Palestine, and former Soviet bloc, such as Russia and Belarus.

Once Cuban control in Venezuela was consolidated, Havana would pressure the members of ALBA to establish extra-continental alliances. Thus, with the Venezuelan support, the Russians and the Chinese in the Hemisphere take root.

Russia grew economically speaking, which allowed President Vladimir Putin to consolidate its geostrategic position by annexing Crimea and Sevastopol to the Russian Federation. It is this same economic and political strength at an international level, as well as the distance from the United States, which has allowed the Eurasian country to approach Latin America.

Other actors have also pounced, such as China and Russia, seeking access to Latin American reserves using Havana and Caracas. In addition, Cuba is considered by European, Chinese and Russian investors as a gateway to Latin American markets.

Therefore, mention should be made of the importance it attributes to the area in a polycentric world by collaborating with Venezuela, Cuba and Nicaragua.

Russia, on the other hand, in addition to approaching it in a commercial way, strengthened political ties in a significant way by giving its support to the political agenda of the different countries with which it negotiated.

Russia, defeated from within during the Cold War, seeks to position itself again to the world, either by helping nations that are problematic for the United States like Syria, or by economically influencing countries traditionally under the North American sphere, such as Nicaragua or Venezuela. The most palpable manifestation of this political interaction has been Vladimir Putin's military agreement with Cuba and Venezuela for $ 4.5 billion, which guarantees ports of both countries for the Russian navy.

Given the lack of presence and projection of the White House, the strategy of replacing the United States in Latin America in political hegemony, in economy, investment, finance and technology has been put in place.

To the extent that the United States faces greater competition from other major powers and has greater difficulty in imposing its designs on other regions of the world, the strategic importance of Latin America and the Caribbean will be evident.

Going further, President Raúl Castro has repeatedly stated that Russia, China, Cuba and Venezuela are strategic partners in terms of oil and military technology.

The Russian-Venezuelan connection is articulated with more than 45 protocols, including a nuclear reactor, a mutual bank with initial capital of $ 12 billion, a Moscow-Caracas direct line and the PDVSA association with the oil consortiums Gazprom, Rosneft, Lukoil to exploit the colossal reserves of the Orinoco, suspending with it commitments with the American oil corporations.

To the numerous tours of Iranian high officials, joined the one of the Russians, with an imposing naval fleet that anchored throughout the Caribbean. Russia's need to import food, because of the sanctions imposed by USA and the EU, is increasing trade with Russia in the region, especially Argentina, Brazil, Ecuador and Chile.

The economic financial crisis within the European Union, the rise of the presence mainly of China, but also India, South Africa, added to Russia, and even Iran in the Middle East, drive a new regionalism in Latin America and the Caribbean much more distant from the United States and Canada, as clear signs of the new times; and weaken US hegemony and challenge its preeminence system to varying degrees.

Taking advantage of the international isolation of Washington, in the wings of this "energy nationalism" Iranian Islamic fundamentalism has entered the continent through the Caracas-Tehran-Havana axis, which has given meaning to the continent's new lefts.

Likewise, Cuba fostered the growing ties of then-Iranian President Mahmoud Ahmadinejad with Venezuela, Nicaragua and Ecuador. Ecuador has been transformed into a financial and Iranian espionage bridge. Its central bank is in the hands of Tehran's financial institutions, and the Iranians travel there without a passport. This creates an extensive subversive network, both against the interests of the United States and Israel, and against any government or institution that is considered "enemy."

With Havana coverage and Venezuelan and Ecuadorian complicity, countless militants and sympathizers of fundamentalist Islamic organizations have entered Latin America and the Caribbean island nations, of which Hezbollah and Hamas are the best known, but not the only ones.

Something very clandestine is the role of special Cuban troops in protecting the deposits and extraction of Venezuelan uranium for the Iranian theocracy atomic weapons program through direct Caracas-Tehran flights. Iran is interested in the Bolivian deposits of uranium and lithium, as this ore will be more important in the development of nuclear energy.

This relationship of Bolivian President Evo Morales reached the point of allowing in official and military bodies the presence and advice of Iranians accused of terrorist attacks against Israeli and Jewish institutions in Argentina.

Is Latin America aware of the danger to its hemispheric security and that of each of its countries, the alliance devised in Havana and consummated by Venezuela with the Iranian fundamentalist?

This design is supported by Presidents Evo Morales, Daniel Ortega and Rafael Correa, in which Cuba participates discreetly, contributing with its experience and its "antiquity" as a subversive and interfering element.

Venezuela and Iran would form a common bank based in Havana, would establish a network of commercial entities in Caracas, signing a military agreement that included the nuclear program, the purchase of armaments manufactured by Cuba and Venezuela and an Iranian training base in Zuata. And all this is involved with PDVSA, which would supply the Iranian gasoline need, in violation of the UN embargo.

This Iranian infrastructure provided by Havana and Caracas would allow it to conceal illegal operations with terrorist organizations in the sub-continent, especially from Margarita Island. In this sense, the Iranians use Venezuelan passports to move and make use of the Ecuadorian banking system to manipulate their finances.

Although China does not yet have global military capability, its inter-hegemonic rivalry with Washington and its growing incidence in the region has led to a readjustment of economic power relations in Southeast Asia.

In fact, it is possible to identify four fronts of international geopolitical China: North Korea,

Iran, Latin America and Africa. In each of them, it weaves differentiated strategies of sub-regional influence, of hegemonic rivalry with the US political agenda.

In addition, the rearrangement of the declining central powers in the international financial bodies and the new structure of indebtedness with China, lead to a new enclave of development and extractive dependency.

China is hungry for raw materials to feed its industries and its population and in Latin America it found a region willing to start an exchange where China aims to replace the US in the long term. In more concrete terms, the link is based on the exchange of Chinese manufactured goods for oil, food and minerals. In other words, it is an exchange between work and land rent. This demand led to a rapprochement with the Latin American region, increasing the prices of exported products (Rosales and Kawayama, 2012: 85).

Sino-Latin American loans demand purchases of Chinese equipment from beneficiary countries and guarantee Chinese energy security during the debt period.

The lines of strategic investments are also in the field of science and technology, as represented by the launch of the Ecuadorian satellite "Pegasus" from a Chinese base, and the Bolivian case with the launch of the satellite "Tupac Katari". In addition to an extensive plan with 64 scholarships to be trained in the management of the satellite at the Chinese Academy of Space.

There are also Chinese companies in Panama and they are involved in the construction of a new canal that would cross Nicaragua. China has been Brazil's largest trading partner for six consecutive years, and at the same time has become the largest trading partner of Chile and Peru and the second largest in Colombia.

Between 2001-2011, trade between both regions grew by 30% per year until reaching the 24 trillion dollars in 2011, which placed China as the second trading partner of the subcontinent, after the United States and the first of strategic countries such as Brazil and Uruguay.

The absence of a specific policy for LA can open more opportunities for China and expand its presence in the area, as it did during the governments of former US presidents Bush and Obama, a period in which exports of the region to China grew more.

In 2012, Xin Jinping said during his visit to Mexico that China's virtual reach extends from Central Asia, with all its mineral and hydrocarbon wealth, to the main navigation routes of the Pacific Ocean.

In his last trip to the Latin American region in 2012, former Chinese Premier Wen Jiabao proposed to double the exchanges and pushed the negotiations for a free trade agreement with the Common Market of the South (Mercosur).

This powerful mercantilism generates an aggressive strategy of commercial intervention, which has begun to threaten the efforts of the United States and several regional actors to control the standards of democratization.

The strategic danger for the United States in Latin America is that China could become a world power model. From a political point of view, the region is important in the diplomatic dispute with Taiwan and as a partner in the search for a more multilateral world.

Drug trafficking

Drug trafficking is an unavoidable topic to understand one of the great problems of our time, not only in our America continent.

If the fight against terrorism is the main issue of national security in the United States, drug trafficking must also be number one along with terrorism. For this reason, Latin America must appear as a region of strategic projection no less important than the Islamic world.

For many years the issue of drugs had been reserved for health experts or public agencies dedicated to the fight against crime. In the 1990s, the subject attracted attention in different social and political sectors.

In several Latin American countries, it was often recognized that the phenomenon of drug trafficking was a threat to national sovereignty and to the security of the State, but today this conception has expanded. In our days, (Riordan, 1991) it figures as a central theme in the Latin America-United States relationship, especially since the end of the Cold War when it became, together with terrorism, the new threat to national security, of the so-called new globalized world.

Most countries in the region have had erratic reactions to drug trafficking. Latin America is facing a new crossroads woven by the paths of illicit drug trafficking (IDT) and other related crimes, with the increase of violence, insecurity and the effects for governability.

The drug business has different phases: production, transport, traffic, wholesale-distribution and retail (by "mules" or dealers). There are many peasants who produce the drug, and many vendors or "kiosks" that sell it. The big business is in the concentration of the intermediate stage. That is why the cartels control the transportation and smuggling that generates net profits between 10,000 and 20,000 dollars per kilogram of heroin or cocaine.

This structure generates wars for the control of traffic and the right to sell to large distributors. They also corrupt the authorities of the territories through which the drug and local networks go. This is the model that is observed on a large scale in Colombia, Venezuela and Mexico.

The thousands of South American migrants on their journey to the United States are the target of blackmail or threats by traffickers to demand the transfer of drugs in their bodies, a more efficient and less expensive mechanism for organized crime.

The Andean region (Colombia, Peru and Bolivia) is the cocaine producing center. Large productions for export of marijuana originate in Mexico, Colombia and Paraguay. The countries that function as producers and/or brokers of the drug are increasing their consumption and initiating domestic production to export and meet domestic demand.

The main cocaine trafficking routes run from the Andean region, especially Colombia, which is the country with the most extensive coca cultivation with half the area devoted to coca bush cultivation worldwide. The percentage of potential cocaine production is more or less: Colombia 60%, Peru 28%, Bolivia 10%.

Some 68,000 Colombian families are engaged in this activity and cultivate in 23 of the 32 provinces of Colombia. Thus, only a third of farmers are growers of other products-

The structure of illegal networks is headed by the cartel or mafia gangsters. Its role is the cultivation, production, design and control of illegal routes of money or drugs by sea and direct remittances to the eastern regions of the United States.

Peru and Bolivia, cocaine-producing countries, their neighbors, and most of the Central American countries serve as places of transshipment. Mexican organizations coordinate the remaining transportation and distribution segments of cocaine in the US. Cocaine is also trafficked to Europe through the Caribbean and, increasingly, through Africa.

Hence, facing this activity face serious security problems such as Colombia, Mexico and the Venezuela Chavist. In the other countries of the Southern Cone and in Brazil, criminal organizations have different degrees of progress, and their ability to destabilize order is related to the balance that maintains with some police very susceptible to being captured or corrupted.

The IDT business is the second in movement of capital in the world, after oil, for the extraordinary profits it provides. It is estimated that illicit drug trafficking internationally generates dividends that exceed $ 320 billion per year.

The presence of secret, unregistered tax haven companies provide services in so-called spaces of secrecy in tax havens (Murphy 2011).

The money laundering system controlled by the Colombian and Mexican cartels is carried out mainly with banks and financial institutions in Colombia, Venezuela, Panama and Florida. In this context, several Caribbean countries, including Cuba, function as tax havens, serve to launder money from drug trafficking, with a tendency to increase, as the sums grow in the market.

A 2008 US Department of State Report said that money laundering as a consequence of all types of illegal transactions ranged between 3 and 5% of world GDP annually, representing an amount of 2.1 to 3.6 trillion dollars.

The economic development achieved by drug trafficking has managed to create links with certain spheres of Latin American political power and this poses a threat to the national security of the United States and the need to combat it outside its borders.

Talking about drug trafficking is, in many ways, talking about the State. Obviously, there is a non-sancta alliance, an understanding based on corruption. Without links to politics, the durability of the drug cartels and the level of expansion and influence they have achieved cannot be explained. The illicit drug trafficking business is an activity that requires irregular interaction with the institutional structure.

The weight of the narco in a country goes beyond corruption: it is an important economic actor, and it can become essential. For all practical purposes, drug trafficking is, in many countries, the lender of last resort for all kinds of activities.

The narcos have known how to build ties with the political classes, especially by financing electoral campaigns and inserting themselves into the clientelist networks that define the political game of many Latin American countries. Some, like that of the campaign of former Colombian President Ernesto Samper, come to light.

There have been times when the Mexican state openly works for the drug traffickers, as in 1985, when the murder of DEA agent Enrique Camarena took place. There are 229 Colombian municipalities without state control where corruption and illegal actors proliferate. Between 16 and 17% of the mayors are managed by posters.

In Latin America, the same politicians who denounce US interventionism and the corruption of governments, use narco-dollars to get elected. In Guatemala, the action of the International Commission against Impunity in Guatemala (CICIG) managed to unveil a criminal network that diverted resources from customs under the leadership of the President of the Republic, Mr. Otto Pérez Molina.

The case of ephedrine became particularly scary in Argentina after it was proven that drugstores that belonged to traffickers had made substantial contributions to the presidential campaign of Cristina Kirchner in 2007. One of the most questioned financial measures of the Kirchner administration was to open a process of money laundering.

Drug trafficking is presented as a new and complex political problem. It requires breaking the legal, social and moral framework of the societies where it operates and needs to resort to extortion, corruption and impunity.

In various nations of the region, drug trafficking emerges as an expression of the direction of their economies, as a mechanism of economic and political power. Latin America is increasingly engaged in the geopolitics of drug trafficking, by uncontrolled violence, institutional corruption and the inefficiency of the agencies responsible for repressing it.

The financial crisis of the 1980s that hit Latin America was largely alleviated by drug-dollars in countries such as Mexico and Colombia. Guatemala, Honduras, Salvador and Nicaragua, because not only are States that depend on remittances that come from the US, but they have become territories of passage of drug trafficking and concentration of urban violence through gangs.

¿Policies of prevention?

A new phenomenon in the region is the growth of domestic markets. Until the 1980s, levels of drug use in the region were relatively low. This new scenario of the drug economy includes larger geographic areas than the States, both at the urban level (marginal neighborhoods in all capitals and major cities), and in distant rural areas (especially in border areas such as the surrounding area). Amazonian).

The abuse of illicit drugs shows alarming figures in the Southern Cone and certain mega cities of South America. Thus, the centers of urban development and modernity of the continent will be surrounded by poverty, illegality and violence. This is the case of the communes in Medellin, the "favelas" of Rio de Janeiro, the towns of Buenos Aires, the satellite city of El Alto in Bolivia, or the port of Callao in Peru, where criminal interests are confronted, poor capacity of police and armed forces.

These spaces outside the state authority grow with the presence of small cartels, gangs and other types of criminal organizations of small size, associated with illicit drug trafficking. Today, licit activities such as construction, tourism, the export sector, are penetrated by drug trafficking.

With illicit money, the purchase of merchandise is financed through exchange markets, so that the foreign currency generated by the IDT does not enter the producing country directly. In this way, the drug business does not benefit the development of the countries, but a way to tie these people into poverty.

No less than 300,000 peasants in the South American Andes participate as raw material suppliers: coca (200,000 has), poppy (1,500 has) and marijuana (not less than 1,000 has). Increasingly, the Amazon region is confronting a progressive and disorderly colonization of illicit economies, involving their ancestral rural societies in this vortex associated with crime (Soberón, 1997).

The governments of Central America, Mexico and Colombia are incapable of facing a problem whose surplus generates millions in excess of their defense spending. In Mexico, the confrontation of drug trafficking groups in various states such as Michoacán, Coahuila, Sinaloa, Chihuahua, Jalisco, Veracruz, Guerrero, among others, is marked by violence that exceeds institutionalist.

With the development of synthetic drugs and the existing facilities for their production, the need for extensive routes or large productions to be stored is eliminated. On the other hand, the infrastructure that must be created in the Latin American countries for the confrontation of the IDT and other related crimes is not capable of regulating the problem of drugs with the speed that new synthetic substances are produced.

The decrease in international economic cooperation of Europe, the United States and international organizations is notorious and leaves the possibilities of alternative development in the Amazonian foothills, except initiatives such as Mérida or Colombia, causing the inefficiency of formal organizations such as Inter-American Drug Control Commission of the OAS or United Nations Office on Drugs and Crime.

In April 2001, Secretary of State Colin Powell accepted before a subcommittee of the United States Congress that market demand was the main incentive for Latin American drug production and trafficking: "it is what causes the problem in Colombia. and in other countries of the Andean region, and therefore we have not only to pursue the offer and resort to interdiction, we must also make sure that we are attacking demand and resorting to treatment for that horrendous problem (News, 04-27-2001).

Both the administrations of Presidents Busch son, and of Barack Obama did not seek to combine a geopolitical and geo-economic approach, opting for a marked military unilateralism. This does not detract from the contribution of the Foreign Deployment Support and Advisory Team (FAST), with experience in Afghanistan, operating in countries of Central America, South America and the Caribbean.

The failure of Plan Colombia, the deadline Andean Regional Initiative ARI, the Plan Mexico or Mérida Initiative demonstrate the incomplete US anti-drug strategy, which rests only in the military pillar, leaving aside economic development programs, employment for prevent marginalized sectors of society from becoming involved in the illicit activity of drugs.

Despite the "Plan Colombia" and the end of the narco-guerrilla, the FARC, since the Colombian governments have not addressed the problems of concentration of land and the existence of local mafias, has prevented solving the structural problems that facilitate the existence of drug trafficking.

The increase in seizures of metric tons of cocaine in the region does not respond to the reduction of the problem. In fact, it is the cost of transportation, where the cartels must invest more in security, expanding their links with legal companies linked to the arms trade and money laundering.

The policies of compulsory eradication of illicit crops are useless until they address the structural problems of rural poverty. The problems of poverty, unemployment and exclusion associated with the use and production of illicit substances need to be resolved.

The decline in cocaine prices since the 1990s and the militarization of the war on drugs have increased the conflicts between the cartels over the control of territories, in an attempt to monopolize the areas to create oligopolies and thus increase their role in the market.

The production of raw materials, the processing, transportation and marketing of drugs, as well as security for their export, includes a greater number of people each day, who find in this business an economic solution to poverty and unemployment. Therefore, the large drug cartels that flourished in Colombia in the 1980s and in Mexico in the 1990s have been modernized and the trend is towards smaller, less visible, less conspicuous cartels.

The peasants who produce the raw materials for these drugs are the ones who receive less benefits, but their standard of living is so basic, that their production is more profitable than that of other agricultural products, in the absence of programs that encourage the eradication of coca leaf and cannabis crops.

The policies of prevention of the production of coca and opium crops and the control of the exportation of drugs, improves the conditions of the peasantry, generates jobs, and reduces the crimes related to the IDT (trafficking of chemical precursors, weapons, people, laundering of money etc.), the incentives that keep the business.

The experiences have reflected the limitations of the anti-drug policy deployed by the US in Latin America. However, no policies are applied to reduce socioeconomic inequalities, which allows the expansion of the middle class, shortening the gap between rich and poor, which would encourage programs to eliminate IDT and other related crimes.

Peru goes through a period of economic growth in the narrow strip of the Peruvian coast (Lima, Trujillo, Arequipa and Piura), while the indigenous and native communities of the

Andean Highlands and the High Jungle, preserve much lower levels of development resulting in both major valleys of coca production associated with drug trafficking.

The difficult sociopolitical situation of Mexico and other structural problems that Mexican society is dragging, leave room for Brazil to take greater leadership to stop the cartel boom that receives so many crimes and victims every day.

The displacement, from the political spectrum of Latin America to the ultra-left and Castro-communism, with its anti-American positions, negatively influenced the counter-narcotics initiatives and the preventive logic that governs its global approach (Jaramillo, 2003-2004).

Colombia

We must consider the difference between the "Pacific" Latin America, supposedly well-disposed to receive the benefits of neoliberal globalization, compared to the "America of the Atlantic", more inclined towards the United States.

The Pacific Alliance, which brings together Chile, Peru, Colombia and Mexico, expresses itself as a project of greater integration of that specific Latin American strip, in the face of the dynamics of the Asian region, considered key in the perspective of global economic growth by concentrating A very important part of international trade flows.

The least mentioned during the last presidential campaign was Colombia, however, the strategic and ideological partner in the USA region could see the ties with its best ally altered, especially because of the fate of the Free Trade Agreement between Colombia and the USA, since in its presidential campaign Trump criticized this type of commercial agreements.

Colombia did not enter the illegal drug business as a passive actor victim of "the vices of the empire". Long before the boom of marijuana and cocaine Colombian drug traffickers were very active in the business. The Colombians introduced an indiscriminate and hitherto unknown violence in the economy of drug trafficking.

In that country, state terrorism, the assassination of trade unionists and the forced displacement of peasants have ruled for decades. Colombia is the largest producer and exporter of cocaine and heroin entering the United States. It is necessary to eradicate the pro-communist danger and the narco-terrorist cartels, creating a new Colombian and continental scenario for democracy and its presidential vision.

During the government of President Alfonso López Michelsen (1974-1978), a cavalier attitude that strengthened Colombia's drug traffickers economically and politically was notorious. The repatriation of capital without asking for its origins and known as "the sinister window" was an official laundry established by the government.

Meanwhile, the elites accepted drug trafficking as a positive thing to irrigate the national economy. This reached the point that a prominent national figure like Fabio Echeverri, for decades president of the ANDI, the powerful industrial union, suggested that drug capitals be legalized so that they pay taxes and legal entrepreneurs, or "good people", had to pay less.

Also, Julio César Turbay Ayala as president (1978-1982), although he militarized "La Guajira", capturing cultivators and mules, however, did not get involved with the Samarian drug traffickers like the Davila Jimeno clan.

Another president, Carlos Lleras Restrepo had the support of drug traffickers, especially among the elite of Santa Marta, and his main fundraiser for the political campaign, was the businessman Gustavo Gaviria González, cousin and right-hand man of drug trafficker Pablo Escobar.

The social and political environment of Colombia has reached such a point that it is virtually impossible to organize a political group that does not contain elements associated with drug traffickers.

Despite the fact that the Colombian State has been successful in dismantling the large drug cartels, illicit crops continue to grow and the business is growing.

The United States transferred to Colombia amounts ranging from $ 10 billion to $ 9 billion per period. Coca cultivation increased to 159,000 hectares in 2015, to 42% increase from 2014.

In addition to the problem of drug trafficking, which is concentrated in the Central America-Mexico corridor from South America to the USA, where 90% of narcotics in the region are transiting north of the continent.

The Colombian countryside became the stronghold of the criminal gangs that control coca production and illegal mining. The Gulf clan, a well-articulated group in the Gulf of Urabá, on the border between Panama and Colombia, was able to develop offensives against the security forces, causing them to lose their lives.

The North Valley cartel, located in intermediate cities and rural areas, seized production centers and corridors. Although this poster suffered blunt blows under the government of Alvaro Uribe.

The Cali cartel headed by the drug lords Rodriguez Orejuela brothers maintains a lower profile and its defense strategy has been to buy the political class, including presidents, and its great national movement of money.

What are the differences between drug traffickers of the likes of Pablo Escobar or Gonzalo Rodríguez Gacha, from the Medellin Cartel, and the profile of the new drug traffickers?

The current narco-traffickers are very different from those of the past; with more education, in small organizations that allow them autonomy even when they serve the posters, with a global vision and low profile; more sophisticated in exporting the drug (in containers or mini-submarines under a ship); with trained mules.

Now the international traffic operations are directed from remote villages or from farms in the middle of the jungle. The private armies of the capos take care of the coca crops, their laboratories, the points of departure and the maritime transport in submersibles to Mexico and other points of arrival of the merchandise.

These "baby posters" are fragmented, inconspicuous organizations that avoid violence and are exclusively dedicated to the operational aspects of the drug business. In this way, only effective cells are in charge of circulating merchandise in international markets through informal networks, which come together to make only one business and new routes that change constantly.

The most used route is not the Caribbean-Florida, now they use the border with Mexico and countries such as Brazil, Argentina, Europe or the United States. Colombians no longer sell directly to the United States, they use criminals, Mexicans, Russians, etc. as intermediaries.

To control international traffic and micro-trafficking, it was necessary to govern peripheral and marginal populations. In this way, Colombian society has been divided between those who are governed by the State and those who, in one way or another, respond to the control of criminals.

Colombia is an emerging country of 29 million people, politically organized in 32 provinces, called departments, and 1101 municipalities.

Colombia is the fourth continental economy; depends on foreign trade with the United States (44% of its exports) and annual aid to its budget of about USA $300 million.

The new scenario in Colombia is key not only for the country but also for the political and economic direction of the Hemisphere. The United States cannot allow, for political and strategic reasons, that Colombia fall into the hands of pro-communist forces supported by

Cuba. That would imply the consolidation of totalitarian regimes and the loss of the continent.

Hence the importance of Colombia for the United States is not only about the fight against drug trafficking, terrorism, but also for being the most influential in Latin America, and prevent the new guerrilla party from establishing its totalitarian vision by exploiting political corruption-mafia and business, and taking advantage of its alliance with Cuba and Venezuela.

The security of Colombia, if maintained as an ally of the USA, could be complicated by the result of the situation created in Venezuela, with the repression of the protests that the democratic opposition deploys to the Castro-Communist government of Nicolas Maduro. Like the existing litigation between the Colombian and Nicaraguan governments on its maritime border in the Caribbean.

The US military presence in Colombia is of particular importance, because of its equidistant geographical location with respect to the two extremes of the American continent and its eventual future use, if it is considered necessary, as a spearhead for Venezuela, the Amazon region and other territories of South America rich in natural resources. At present, the Pentagon has seven powerful bases in Colombia.

Electoral fraud in countries like Venezuela and Colombia is always prepared many months in advance to remain in government. The Colombian and Venezuelan people have experienced this electoral fraud, with Chavez, Maduro and Santos.

While there is talk of legality, it exists without rights, because they are countries where there is no true democracy, especially because of the enormous influence exerted by Castro's Cuba.

The administrations of Cuba-Venezuela and much of Colombia are aimed at safeguarding the narco project.

The new revised Peace agreement endorsed by the Congress is pending decision by the constitutional court, because of the polarization of the Colombian people.

Most of, Many of the Colombian people think that the peace agreement benefits the violent and the lawless, rewarding them with: lands, productive projects, non-refundable seed capital, subsidized financing.

The middle class against high unemployment, also, many of the young people who have lived through these five decades are now adults without employment or business opportunities.

There is something that the American administrations must consider in the case of Colombia; and is that lately, especially under President Juan M. Santos, has manifested positions that are articulated with a concerted regional stance supporting the Cuban communist government. This has been observed more recently at the Summits of the Americas from 2009 to 2015.

President Santos has distanced himself from the American political positions developed by his predecessor Alvaro Uribe and has offered himself as a mediator in Cuba, trying to emulate the former Argentinian President Arturo Frondizi, who sought to mediate between John F. Kennedy and Fidel Castro, prior to the expulsion of Havana from the OAS in January 1962.

Undoubtedly, former president Uribe's positions are much more in line with President Trump's reality than President Juan Manuel Santos, who was a ruler very close to President Obama.

Therefore, the relationship established in the coming years with the different political forces in Colombia will determine the direction of relations with the United States. A weakened President Santos after the defeat of the referendum for Peace could open the doors to the positions of senator Uribe.

The historical problem of violence in the country and the climate generated by drug trafficking demand solutions of social and political order that Colombia must face. In addition to the agrochemical and biological eradication, alternative development programs are needed for the areas in Tumaco, Nariño (the municipality with the most coca), assisted with a new institutional design that supports small and medium agricultural producers and supplants the 96,000 hectares of illicit crops with alternative economies.

The Judicial Power and the Public Prosecutor's Office should be strengthened; develop a thorough campaign to prevent and control money laundering; of social prevention; of treatment and rehabilitation of the addict, and security policies. Also, identify and dismantle the financing systems of organized crime organizations.

Recently the defense minister and the military leadership met with the deputy assistant secretary of state for US anti-narcotics issues. W. W., William Brownfield, and the ambassador of that country in Bogotá, Kevin Whitaker, to present the plan of Colombia to eradicate areas of coca cultivation.

But the Colombian state does not have the financial muscle to establish new crops and distribute land, even in the 8 departments controlled by the narco-guerrilla of the FARC.

The political destiny of Colombia, the consolidation of its democratic and market economy scheme is overshadowed by drug trafficking, corruption and the Castro-communist ideology of the Farc. That is why an electoral platform and a clear political message of a presidential figure are the alternatives to face and overcome such obstacles.

Within the Colombian political altarpiece, one of the personalities that meets such requirements is the Senator and presidential candidate Alejandro Ordoñez Maldonado. Lawyer, Honoris Causa in Political Science, which has always stood out for its campaign against corruption.

Ordoñez, senator since 2008 and general prosecutor of the Nation from 2009 to 2013, in June of 2017 registered his candidacy for the presidency of Colombia for the movement "La Patria de Pie", with which he got 2.2 million signatures.

With a government program and a management style that recalls that of US President Donald Trump, Ordóñez opposes abortion; together with the majority of Colombians, he rejects the Havana peace accords with the FARC.

Ordóñez is committed to the protection of Colombian families; in the development of public policies to prevent crime with the support of the National Police and other institutions.

It also declares that it will pursue drug trafficking throughout the production and distribution chain and will reinforce the security of the Colombian countryside.

In economic terms, it plans to relieve taxes on businesses and consumers; lower the income tax from 33% to 30%; return the VAT to 16%; and decrease the existing parallel bureaucracy to obtain a fiscal balance.

Socially, it hopes to maintain a free education system, strengthen schools in basic sciences; I will expand pension coverage; attend to peasant families; increase the budget to advance in the production technology and improve the process of industrialization of the Colombian countryside.

FARC: The Narco-guerrilla

On August 27, 2016, while in Havana the peace in Colombia was discussed, the government of the United States announced that he had discovered an illegal network of the FARC in Switzerland, of Colombians living in that country, and two companies in Zurich: Latin Shop and Adolfo Fonnegra Espejo Trading & Investment, which according to John E. Smith, director of OFAC, facilitated the guerrilla services of remittances from abroad and access to the international financial system, covering up a washing plot.

In its annual reports on the Situation of Terrorism in Europe (TE-SAT 2010 and 2011), Europol pointed out the links between the FARC and the Spanish terrorist group ETA, whose coordinations were made on social networks. That agency tracked frequent trips of "ETA members" to Venezuela for explosives courses for the guerrillas.

The FARC considers Europe an area of strategic interest, sending representatives to some member states. Its mission includes the creation of cells to facilitate drug trafficking and the purchase of weapons

In the computer seized from "Raúl Reyes" (2008) it was evident that the representative of the guerrilla in Oceania was the Chilean Vlaudin Rodrigo Vega (Carlos Vlaudin), according to the

Treasury. The press in Australia, a country that does not consider the FARC terrorists, has reviewed its activities since 2001.

One of its connections favored by Cuba is with the army of Guinea Bissau, on the west African coast, destination of the clandestine routes that cross the Atlantic by water and air, from Venezuela and Brazil.

In 2013, according to the newspaper El Colombiano, the DEA conducted an undercover operation that uncovered an agreement between the guerrillas and the military of that country. The DEA established that once the drugs reach the West African coast (Guinea Bissau, Nigeria and Ghana), they follow a route to the north of the continent (Libya, Morocco and Algeria), heading to the Mediterranean. The drug travels in caravans escorted by local illegal groups, including Al Qaeda.

This became clear in 2009, when three terrorists were arrested in Ghana carrying cocaine Fariana Idris Abdelrahman, one of the captives, who confessed to the DEA that Al Qaeda and the FARC had common goals, including "the anti-American cause." As stated in a report of the Department of State.

In a report submitted to the Foreign Affairs Committee of Congress (2011), entitled "Emerging Threats in the Western Hemisphere," Daniel L. Glaser, Deputy Assistant Secretary of the Treasury Department, said that Central America, in particular Guatemala and Panama, was a center for money laundering. One of the effects of tightening regulations in Mexico was the displacement of smuggling of cash and money laundering activities in these two countries.

In Panama, the FARC has a large cell and is considered by the local Public Force as a drug trafficking group. The authorities of the isthmus have calculated that at least 400 guerrillas move across the border, crossing the jungles of the Darien to install camps and drug routes. They take advantage of rivers like the Balsa, Turia, Pavarandó and Tuquesa, not only to transport drugs, but lumps of money and gold.

The FARC considers the government of President Daniel Ortega as "sympathetic" to its movement and uses its territory for political, economic and leisure activities. The president has received them officially in Managua, despite the protest of the Colombian Foreign Ministry. The most illustrative case was in 2008, when he met with the then guerrilla leader Alfonso Cano.

That same year, President Ortega granted asylum to the FARC delegate in Ecuador, Nubia Calderón de Trujillo (Esperanza), after she survived the bombing in which Raúl Reyes died. In 2008, the Nicaraguan newspaper La Prensa also published a report based on emails found on the computer of this guerrilla leader, which showed that President Ortega was working for the government of Libya to make a loan of US $ 100 million to the FARC.

There has also been the training of Paraguayan terrorists by the FARC of the

Paraguayan People's Army (EPP), an armed movement that kidnaps and extorts.

The official support of the FARC in the Colombian government media is known. During the government of Alvaro Uribe, officials Juan Manuel Santos, now president and then defense minister and Sergio Jaramillo vice minister, collaborated clandestinely with the FARC. This was reported by General Javier Rey and more recently made by Colonel Hernan Mejia Gutiérrez in his book "I'm not going to Kneel."

Castro-Communism

Any formulation of the world major political and military powers policy concerning the fight against terrorism would be incomplete without in-depth analysis and understanding the nature and extent of Cuba's terrorist and subversive activities that had taken place out of the public view.

You cannot fight terrorism without taking in account Castro´s Cuba. You cannot understand terrorism without studying Cuban last five decades. You cannot stop terrorism ignoring the dealings of Havana. But ironically, Cuba's campaign of violence is not actually of great concern to many countries, including the United States, a big mistake.

Cuba is clearly not the sole source of violence and instability in the third world, but was the most important one and is the most experience, and its activities had militarized and internationalize what would otherwise be local conflicts. A country-by-country examination during the last five decades of Cuba's activities in Latin America, the Caribbean, Africa and countries in the Middle East makes clear that Cuba has campaigned to promote actual insurgencies and terrorism.

Unlike the attention the subject has received in the West, Cuban global interaction with terrorist and revolutionary groups has generated relatively little research. Because the Cuban government carefully guards hard data regarding its subversive and terrorist activities, Cuban scholarly research on the subject has not surfaced.

Throughout the twentieth century, both with the Cuban Democratic Republic and with the Castro-Communist regime, US policy towards Cuba has been an element of significance for the design of politics towards the region, sometimes explicitly, others implicitly.

Moreover, the scarcity of research conducted by LatinAmerican themselves deprives us of a valuable mirror, in which we could view both the extent and effectiveness of Cuban subversive initiatives in the region as well as Cuba's undermine to a major concern in the case of Latin America and Middle East: stability. Unfortunately, one is left to wonder that this is because they find Cuba's role in those regions less significant than their counterparts in the West: another big mistake.

Most works on the subject previously tended to focus on Cuba's relations with the Soviet Union in order to explain Cuba's objectives as well as the seeming degree of independence Cuba enjoys in those areas This level of analysis is used mainly because Cuba's relatively wide international projection is unusual for a country with such limited resources. It is generally accepted that decades ago, in Africa, Latin America or the Middle East Cuba was neither a proxy of the Soviet Union nor a totally autonomous actor.

Despite the lack of a comprehensive view of Cuba's involvement in other continents, this is perhaps the key factor that explains its visibility on the international scene. Contact with Africa, Latin America and the Middle East, one of the most significant initiatives of the Cuban Revolution, has extended the scope and reach of Cuba's international relations further than ever before.

Apart from the major powers, and the extinct Soviet Union no other Latin American country not even Brazil which also has a dynamic international policy has yet matched Cuba's far-reaching commitments.

There is not any country in the world, not a political elite, or a head of state during the XX century that could match the terrorist and subversive projection of Castro´s brother Cuba; not even the extinct Soviet Union, or yet the Libya of mercurial Muamar Khadafy, or the Assad dynasty of Syria, or the eccentrics of North Korea, or the arachnid movements of Yasser Arafat PLO.

None of these countries, not any of these movements, no one of those terrorist bosses deployed such a vast organization, limitless material resources, intelligence mechanisms, trained personnel, targets and policies than Havana´s Castro brother terrorist and subversive actions.

In places whose primary needs are for economic development, social equity, and greater democracy, Cuba compounded the existing problems by encouraging violence.

Havana's terrorist activities rarely make headlines and nearly always avoid serious inquiry. The Cuban leadership has avoided any mention of the subject even in their propaganda, style that contrasts sharply with the Middle East terrorist organizations.

Cuba has worked to unite traditionally splintered radical groups behind a commitment to armed struggle with Cuban advice and material assistance. Cuba has trained committed cadres in urban and rural guerrilla warfare to assume power by force; supplied or arranged for the supply of weapons; encouraged terrorism in the hope of provoking indiscriminate violence and repression; used military aid and advisors to gain influence over violent factions and radical governments.

Cuba has provided advise, safe haven, communications, training, and some financial support to several violent international organizations. Cuba is quick to exploit legitimate grievances for its own ends. But its strategy is not based on appeals to the "people." Instead, Cuba concentrates on developing self-proclaimed "vanguards" committed to violent action.

Cuba´s influence in Central America, the Caribbean, the southern cone of Africa, and the Gulf of Aden is comparable only to that exercised by Unites States.

We may, therefore, assume that Fidel and Raul Castro's proactive foreign policy and his ever-increasing ties to tile the former Soviet Union and actual Venezuela are directly related to their needs to consolidate their power base at home.

Sponsorship of terrorism is a longstanding and major part of Cuba's foreign policy. Training and supporting small bands of terrorists, often with third country weapons (such as from Vietnam) costs relatively little. The American anti-terrorist campaign was never directed at Cuba, but at more obvious offenders.

The formulation of the Alliance for Progress, launched by assassinated President John F. Kennedy, explicitly made clear that it was intended to push for limited reforms to prevent the advance of other communist revolutions.

Despite its long involvement in promoting violence, Havana has never been spotlighted as have Iran's Ayatollah Khomeini, been more dangerous than them because the U.S. public is not aware of it.

Concerning the US. the Cuban strategy has been the creation of anti-capitalist totalitarian states in Latin America and the promotion of subversive and terrorist movements in the Hemisphere. Also, the diffusion of U.S. military power away from Cuba and to other geographical areas. The erosion of the Inter-American defense system.

The plans and programs of assistance to the counterinsurgency complemented the North

American projection towards the continent. Likewise, the Republican wave led by President Ronald Reagan in the 1980s propelled the Caribbean Basin Initiative (CBI) and assistance programs to Central America to reverse the rise of pro-communist guerrilla movements.

Likewise, those who consider that Cuba's foreign policy is totally reactive to the coercion of the United States fail to explain the former's involvement in Angola, Ethiopia, Venezuela, Nicaragua, and Ecuador at a critical time of wide-ranging negotiations with the latter.

In addition, more recent factors to consider include: the political instability in Latin America; the lack of U.S. interest in Latin America and Africa; the US. military problems in Afghanistan and Iraq; and the global economic crisis, among others.

As part of this policy, support was given to the armed opposition in Nicaragua to overthrow the communist Ortega government.

The US administration knew the design of Cuba to generalize communism in Central America, to the point that even then Secretary of State Alexander Haig proposed to go to the alleged source of conflicts and threatened a devastating military intervention against Cuba.

From that moment, in 1982, the Castro-communist government was included in the list of countries that sponsor terrorism in the framework of the Central American conflict.

Any on-going inquiry in to Cuba's future involvement in subversion, terrorism and US destabilization, especially now in Latin America, must include new factors and perspectives that have been, heretofore, largely overlooked by most of the international specialist on terrorism and intelligence agencies.

Among Cuba's wide-ranging activities in Africa, Latin America and the Middle East some more successful than others military involvement and civilian internationalist cooperation figure as the most prominent. These two aspects of Cuban activities have involved guerrilla training to "liberation movement" combatants, the deployment of thousands of soldiers, as well as the provision of teachers, doctors, technicians, construction workers, etc., to several Latin America, Africa and Middle East countries.

Cuban anti-USA quest

It should be emphasized that in addition to violence and terrorism, Cuba have been for more than five decades, the most vocal and active proponents of anti Americanism. Despite the collapse of the Soviet Union, Castro continues to undermine U.S. policies in the Middle East in several ways: a) by portraying U.S. actions and diplomacy in the region as those of an aggressor, seeking to impose hegemony by force, particularly in Iraq and the perpetration of unjustified economic sanctions on Iraq and Iran; b) by portraying the U.S. as the main obstacle to a peaceful settlement of the Israel/Arab conflict; and c) by discrediting U.S. policies and seeking support for Cuba at the U.N. (Suchlicki, 2001).

Most of the covert operations in support of this strategy are planned and coordinated by several intelligence departments that brought together the expertise of the Cuban military and the General Directorate of Intelligence into operations that included secret training camps, networks for covert movement of personnel and materiel between Cuba and abroad, and sophisticated propaganda support.

The bureaucratic apparatus directly responsible for foreign policy, and legal and illegal policy (except the MINFAR), has 8,000 to 10,000 persons. He is in charge of diplomatic, consular, trade, military, technical, and public liaison, as well as intelligence agents; the promotion of subversion; guerrilla training; propaganda; front organizations; illegal trade; contraband; drugs; and special commands with deadly missions.

Cuba's espionage apparatus (the DGI), one of the largest and most efficient on the planet, with more than 10,000 spies, analysts, technical personnel, etc., has been active on a global scale. Cuban intelligence officers are present in every Cuban diplomatic mission encouraging terrorism and any kind of violence in the hope of provoking indiscriminate belligerence and repression and generalized legitimacy and attract new converts.

During the Cold War, the DGI joined the KGB for the gathering of economic, technological, and military information from U.S., European, and NATO sources. Specialized Cuban well trained agents were planted undercover in the United States, Spain, Italy, and Canada.

Despite important changes and developments in Latin America and the Caribbean since the Cuban Revolution and later during the new pro-communist cycle initiated with President Hugo Chávez in December 1998, the region has continued to be considered as a zone relatively secure geography by North American strategic planners, based on the perception that threats to the vital interests of the United States are not existing at present.

Here lies the main cause of its low priority in that country's foreign policy. Let us not forget that in our hemisphere there are several countries that hate the United States, or at least they do not want this country as an ally.

Communist Cuba is at the top of the list of enemy countries. The Cuban regime does not disguise its sympathy for the international terrorists who have declared war on the United States. Cuba has spies in the country. And let's not forget that the Cuban government has used its population as a weapon against the United States.

The target of the DGI in the U.S. has been the White House, the CIA, the FBI, the Department of State, the Congress, the Immigration Department and the anti-Castro organizations. As for Western Europe, the intelligence service has been the target, namely that of France, Germany, Italy, Spain and Great Britain. The DGI has accomplished its objectives through the recruitment of governmental officials and agents and contact with citizens, universities, and the press.

Panama has been used as a regular transit point for the Hemisphere to and from military training in Cuba, especially as a transit point for Colombian guerrillas coming from Havana. Cuba has taken advantage of Mexico's open society and its extensive presence there to carry out support activities for insurgencies in other countries. Mexico is a principal base for Cuban contacts logistical support, and international activities.

And during the Vietnam War, Castro dispatched his henchmen to Hanoi to viciously torture U.S. POWs as documented by the historians Rochester and Riley (January 15, 2013).

After the fall of the Berlin Wall, a meeting took place in 1990 between the trade unionist and then president of Brazil, the Communist Luiz Ignacio Lula da Silva with Fidel Castro Ruz. There it is agreed to convene in Sao Paulo, Brazil, all communist, socialist and radical left-wing political organizations to redefine the new tactics and forms of struggle for the seizure of power in all Latin American countries.

Hence the name of Forum of Sao Paulo. To Fidel Castro's proposal the strategy would be a "democratic" socialism to appease suspicions and be able to participate in elections and then establish the regime permanently.

The Sao Paulo Forum, conceived by Havana for the entire left, had to use a "politically correct" neo-communist language to confront democracy, Christianity and capitalism in America.

The new design of Havana promoted the transition to a communist model without having to resort to violent means to achieve this transition.

Thus, it was designed to build a dual power in Nicaragua, Venezuela, Bolivia and Ecuador to avoid an eventual coup of the state and to seek the possibility for Castro-communist elites to infiltrate these state structures and generate changes both within the state and outside.

The weakness of political democracy in Latin America is that it is plagued with clientelism and suffers a huge lack of awareness of institutionalization. Therefore, the expression in vogue of being classified as democracies of low intensity.

Havana does not seek "revolutionary" regimes through insurgency; now it is the petrodollars and their espionage that constitute the winning amalgam. It takes advantage of voters' frustration to choose messianic caudillos by making manipulated elections that allow a view of "legitimacy" to international opinion.

To the two years the Venezuelan colonel, Hugo Chávez raised in arms to take the power in Venezuelan it. Then, Daniel Ortega consolidated his clique in Nicaragua; this was followed by Evo Morales in Bolivia and then Ecuador. And, for Colombia, it was proposed that the FARC promote a negotiation that will allow them to take power by means of elections.

Cuba was the promoter of the "authoritarian policies" and "state control of the economy" deployed by the Venezuelan government led by dictator Hugo Chávez; Who for years worked to subvert democracy in his own country and across the region. Let us not forget Nicaragua, where the communist Daniel Ortega rules tyrannically, with the support of Cuba and Russia, although at present he faces a democratic armed opposition that has received neither international recognition nor support.

The problem of Venezuela taken advantage of by Castro-communism is basically the same scheme that Havana has designed for all Latin America. The propaganda of Havana has meant that in these countries the right to citizenship is confused with the right to nationality. Havana emphasizes taking advantage of the vote is universal and direct, to promote a populism that ends in the Cuban communist version.

Simultaneously, and in line with the Forum of Sao Paulo, a no-man's territory was consolidated between Brazil, Argentina and Paraguay, the so-called "Triple Frontier". It would be a center with strong participation of the Cuban intelligence services, to support Islamic terrorist groups, taking advantage of the large Arab immigrant community that is there.

In the "Triple Frontier" there is presence of both HizbAlláh and Al-Qaeda, as a zone suitable for sleeping cells. In addition to being a base for terrorists, the absence of the law in that region makes it an ideal corridor for smuggling, for drug trafficking, forgery of documents, etc.

The permeability of the borders between Peru, Chile, Bolivia, Brazil, Paraguay and Argentina has facilitated a high level of activity of the Mexican and Colombian narco, with close ties with HizbAlláh.

Both the Sao Paulo Forum and the "Triple Frontier" are a dangerous mix, a major threat to hemispheric security.

The presence of Islamic transnational groups in Latin America, and especially HizbAlláh, has been under discussion for several years. Its cells are made up of expatriates and descendants of Syrians and Shiite Lebanese, who are supported by the policies of the "Bolivarian governments" of the continent, essentially the Sao Paulo Forum and Cuba.

The Castro-Chávez Government of Venezuela and the Colombian FARC have provided resources and trafficked influences to financially benefit HizbAlláh operations, such as drug trafficking and money laundering in line with Mexico's criminal cartels. Likewise, the support Iran gives to HizbAlláh in Peru is part of its strategy to gain a presence in Latin America.

Both Iran and its extensions in HizbAllah and Al-Qaeda have declared war on Jewish communities in the area, especially in Argentina and Peru.

Castro-Chavism

Venezuela has strategic reserves of vital importance for the North American and world biotechnology industry; abundant reservoirs of drinking water and the presumption about the existence of usable minerals for the radioactive industry possess in abundance, oil and gas.

Geopolitically speaking, Venezuela is a key point to guard, as head of the continent, all of the Caribbean and observatory towards the Atlantic Ocean, Central America and the provinces that leeward and windward possesses the European Union in the Caribbean north.

The Bolivarian Revolution of Venezuela, the citizen revolution in Ecuador, the multicultural State of Bolivia have joined Cuba to form a solid political alliance to confront Washington.

In the absence of a common United States security strategy with the countries of the continent, the result has been the lack of definition of the concept of external danger. It is evident that not only has the American democratic model been scorned but that alarming extra-hemispheric military, technological and economic alliances have been promoted.

That is the reason that has facilitated to Cuba, in this first part of Century XXI, to use of the vast oil resources of Venezuela; consuming a lethal axis with the despots of Bolivia, Ecuador and Nicaragua, promoting the Iran of the ayatollahs and exercising of continental window for the access of Russia and China.

And this does qualify as the most formidable threat to the interests and national security of the United States on this continent, hampering the fight against terrorism, drug trafficking and worsening immigration problems.

Throughout its political history, the Latin American sub-continent has been defined on two axes: Cuba-Colombia and Argentina-Brazil. For a couple of decades, the Cuba-Venezuela pole has become strategic in the face of Washington's indolence.

In 1959 Fidel Castro proposed to the then Venezuelan president Romulo Betancourt to erect a political-oil alliance not only to seize the continent but to confront the United States. But President Betancourt refused and an angry Castro unleashed guerrilla violence.

After the debacle of the Soviet bloc, the Castro´s brother evicted his old plan, this time with the complicity of the Venezuelan "left", which demanded that he give unrestricted support in the following presidential elections to a former coup: Hugo Chavez.

Havana's anonymous colonel, Hugo Chavez, won the 1998 elections thanks to a team of Cuban computer experts and the venomous pocket of Havana.

Castro immediately convinced Chávez to buy the Caribbean and African countries' votes with petro-dollars, to first ensure a comfortable majority in the OAS, neutralizing any future action by Washington and to have broad support in the UN to hypnotize Europe.

Cuba and Venezuela by Hugo Chavez and Nicolas Maduro have questioned Washington's peace and mediation initiatives and organized the first World Social Forum in Porto Alegre as a space against the FTAA. This was followed by the support of pro-Castro-Communist regimes in Nicaragua, Bolivia, and Ecuador, changing the correlation of forces in Latin America.

Venezuela colonization

The key to understanding Cuban control in Venezuela is the presence of some 60,000 Cubans in areas ranging from the military, security, health, education, sports, communications, and so on.

The main component is the permanent Cuban General Staff in Fort Tiuna, in direct contact with the Havana Operations Center, and consists of 2 generals, 4 colonels, 5 lieutenant colonels and 25 junior officers who direct 8 Cuban battalions.

In addition, this EM has under its immediate command the Barquisimeto fort and the air bases of Carrizal, Apure and Maracaibo, and supervises and plans all the operations of the Armed Forces of Venezuela.

An important part of the Cuban military framework are its senior officers who operate directly in the headquarters of the 6 Venezuelan infantry divisions located in Maracaibo, Caracas, San Cristóbal, Maracay, Apure and Ciudad Bolívar.

With great skill, the Cuban Military Counter Intelligence (CIM) has organized its Venezuelan counterpart and has infiltrated the main military facilities, in the Ministry of Defense, the Venezuelan General Staff, the Air Force, the Navy and the National Guard.

For its part, Cuban Intelligence operates in the Venezuelan Foreign Ministry and embassies. And there are parallel structures of Cubans that replicate and interfere with the main Venezuelan state institutions. For example, the key oil infrastructure, such as the Centro Planta, is being guarded by the Cuban Special Troops that only respond to Havana.

But the great interference is that of the Cuban generals in their character of presidential adviser from Miraflores presidential palace, for the operations of urban repression and the handling of the internal political crises.

About 150 highly trained Cubans are in charge of the various rings of the personal security of President Nicolas Maduro, as well as the perimeter of Miraflores. In addition to maintaining devices of Cuban Special Troops in neuralgic points of Caracas.

To this are added the Cuban military detachments that guard the Iranian uranium extraction plant of the Upper Orinoco, Esmeralda area, and the Port Ordaz used for transportation. There are also prominent Cuban military personnel in the state of Cojeda, in Port Cabello, on the Colombian border, especially in Guasdalito and Apure.

The degree of Cuban intervention reaches the orbital control of the Venezuelan satellite "Venesat-1" which covers the continent. To this is added the submarine fiber optic cable that links both countries, guaranteeing a greater supervision of the Venezuelan strategic areas.

This has allowed manipulation of Venezuelan elections from Cuba which manages the registration of personal identifications, including electoral votes. The palmaria test was the last presidential election where Nicolás Maduro was elected by the count and result of the votes processed in Havana.

The growing instability in Venezuela after Chavez's death, the weakening of Brazil after the fall of the Workers' Party, the Argentina of Mauricio Macri, and the growing hand of President Raúl Castro in the Colombian crisis, draw a scenario in which the United States must act.

Venezuelan opposition leaders grouped in the MUD - among them Enrique Capriles, Antonio Ledesma, Leopoldo López and Corina Machado, who have sought a dialogue between government and opponents, need the unrestricted support of the United States.

The ultra-left has not been able to present results in their positions, which have not settled in any country of the continent, nor in Europa.

The main failure of the ultra-left has been not understanding the character of the current historical epoch, the error of its visions and the recurrent impotence to construct alternatives. This occurs in Brazil, Argentina, Venezuela, Nicaragua, Ecuador, Bolivia, Uruguay. Nor do they manage to grow in other countries, such as Mexico, Peru, Chile or Colombia.

Social welfare and pension systems have not been sustainable. The leaders of Venezuela,

Nicaragua, Ecuador, Bolivia, failed to fulfill democratic traditions by expanding their mandates or removing boundaries and creating clientelism networks to co-opt independent public institutions.

But the wall of leftist governments in Latin America threatens to crack due to corruption and poor economic policy decisions. In general, these pro-Communist leaders fail to create diversified economies capable of supporting economic cycles, with their ups and downs.

What is at stake here is the political nullity of the United States in the continent to consolidate a group of like-minded countries with the posture of the alleged Castroist transcendentalism as "21st Century Socialism".

The key to the current regime of Nicolás Maduro, as seen, lies in the Cuban military structure that operates within Venezuelan territory; disappearing this presence, the authoritarian Caracas regime would crumble like a tower of cards.

The Nicaraguan Sandinista

The Sandinista regime in Nicaragua is a Castro-communist dictatorship who has transform already in a dynasty. In addition to facing an electoral opposition also meets an armed opposition in the north of the country.

Sebastián Marroquin, son of the beleaguered cartel leader of Medellin, Pablo Escobar Gaviria, said in an interview with CNN that his family lived in Nicaragua in the eighties and that they received more protection from the authorities than in Panama.

At that time President Daniel Ortega and the Sandinista National Liberation Front (FSLN) governed in Nicaragua. With the approval of the Sandinista Pablo Escobar with the help of the Nicaraguan and Cuban military, and the North American pilot Barry Sea, he set up the drug trafficking routes in Nicaragua.

With President Ortega, Nicaragua has become a legal paradise for transnational narco-crime. And the penetration of drug trafficking has spread to almost all the institutions of the Nicaraguan State.

According to what was published by InSight Crime on August 31, 2012, the protected witness at the trial of alleged drug trafficker Henry Fariñas provided gray details of how Fariñas' organization would smuggle cocaine for Mexican groups like the Michoacan Family, and ruthlessly dispose of drug mules suspected of stealing the cargo.

Fariñas testified that many Nicaraguan drug mules, used to smuggle small amounts of cocaine into Guatemala, ended up dead if they were blamed for stealing their illicit cargo. In his statements, Fariñas involved senior officials of the National Police of Nicaragua and magistrates of the Supreme Court.

In its publication of July 2012, "InSight Crime" points out capo Amauri Carmona Morelos in charge of laundering money at the Managua nightclub "Mr. Sponge ", which was used as a meeting center to negotiate the transportation and purchase of the drug; all with the knowledge of President Daniel Ortega.

Nicaragua manages organized crime; the business deals are made with representatives from the state. In other words, Nicaragua is the regulates the drug trade. The United States Embassy in Managua made much the same claims in a secret 2006 diplomatic cable published by WikiLeaks.

The cable alleges that President Daniel Ortega and his party used money from international drug traffickers to finance political campaigns.

President Ortega reformed the constitution to allow for indefinite re-elections. Most recently, in a coup of grace to any semblance of democracy, he had taken away the legal representation of the opposition to manipulate the 2016 elections.

The Electoral Court controlled by the Sandinista Front makes electoral farces possible, to the point that the European Union had already criticized what it called the "opacity" of the electoral system.

The opposition has expressed that elections supervised by international entities, including the Organization of American States (OAS), are the only method to remove Daniel Ortega from power.

The opposition was excluded from the elections last November 2016, and more than 70% of the electorate did not vote, which illegitimatizes Ortega's presidential couple as president and his wife as vice president.

In the USA, the "NICA Act" (Conditionality to Nicaraguan Investments), approved by the House of Representatives, seeks to prevent Nicaragua from having access to international funds until it promotes democratic reforms, guaranteeing free elections and supervised by external observers.

President Ortega, after his electoral victory in 2006, decided to "make a proposal to the Russian Federation to help us replace the combat equipment that was already defeated." This managed was carried out through Cuba obtaining the political support, armament and Russian technology.

Since 2008, the Sandinista regime has openly supported Russia in its position vis-a-vis the separatist regions of Abkhazia and South Ossetia, which in 1991 and 1992 declared their independence from Georgia. Only Russia, Nicaragua and Venezuela have recognized the independence.

In July 2014 President Vladimir Putin paid a visit to Nicaragua, the first of a Russian president to the Central American country. On that occasion, the commitment was made to rearm the Nicaraguan army with the financing by Russia of a military training center.

Russia's ambassador to Nicaragua, Nikolay Mikhailovich Vladimir, told Nicaraguan newspaper The Press that Russia is interested in getting closer to Latin America. "The world is much more complex; in fact, it's a multipolar world and one of the most dynamic poles is Latin America, and Nicaragua, as a Latin American that is a member of the Community of Latin American and Caribbean States (CELAC) integration and regional integration process plays a huge role.

President Ortega has become an operator for Russian interests, he has benefited economically from this exchange, receiving economic and military support, in exchange for Russia's strategic and territorial presence. Nicaragua is becoming a military dependence with Russia, who have declared their desire to have bases in Cuba, Venezuela and Nicaragua.

The Russian military training center, according to President Ortega will benefit not only Nicaraguan military, but also other unspecified countries. Russia is facilitating all kinds of weapons and ships; There have even been talks of purchasing aircraft.

The contract for military assistance and weapons consisted of delivery of 50 T-72B1 tanks, 12 anti-aircraft defenses systems ZU-23-2, two Molnia missile carriers 1241.8, four Mirazh-14310 patrol boats, one lot of Tiger-GAZ-2330 armored vehicles, two MI-17V-5 helicopters and several Yak-130 combat and training aircraft. All this accompanied by the purchase of 8 MiG-29 for US $ 235 million.

In 2014, Russian Defense Minister Gen. Sergey Shoigú announced the installation of Russian bases in Venezuela, Cuba and Nicaragua for the equipping of its air force in Latin America. Likewise, Russian Foreign Minister Sergey Lavrov stated that Russia would provide the military security in the Canal Zone of Nicaragua built by the Chinese.

Russian Airborne Forces carried out military maneuvers in Nicaragua, taking advantage of the presence of Russian Navy ships, which arrived from Cuba via Panama

Russia legislators passed a draft legislation to establish a network of satellite navigation stations in Nicaragua. Moscow established a station of the Glonass Satellite Monitoring System, which will provide information for various services. The base operates from Nejapa, in the outskirts of Managua.

The construction of a Russian espionage base in Nicaragua has returned to prominence in Central America. This operation is part of

Moscow's efforts to increase its military and intelligence activities in the Western Hemisphere.

Between July 1 and December 31, 2016, a unit of 424 Russian special forces was also stationed for the purpose of training the Nicaraguan troops, assisted by ships and aircraft of the Armed Forces of the Russian Federation.

USA and the countries of the region should be concerned, as Nicaragua offers a beachhead for Russia to expand its intelligence and naval intrusion, while militarily consolidating Nicaragua's pro-communist regime.

China's investment to build the transoceanic canal will be about $ 50 billion; the largest infrastructure ever built, connecting the Pacific Ocean with the Atlantic and crossing Nicaraguan territory from east to west, and will be a competition to the Panama Canal.

While it would supply Asia with more cargo from Latin America, especially Brazil, the Canal provides China with strategic access very close to North America, a geopolitical movement against the USA, weakening its political influence in the continent and causing a severe blow to its prestige.

If Panama is already expanding its Canal to facilitate the passage of larger merchant ships and oil tankers, what is the objective of building next to it another Canal? Behind the plans for this construction there is a geopolitical interest of China, which would strengthen its influence in the region and seek to extract Latin America from the Panama Canal, closely interlinked with the USA.

The USA retains the right to intervene in the Panama Canal in case of conflict, and controls and influences the main maritime and commercial routes: the Panama Canal, the Suez Canal, Singapore, Gibraltar, etc. Therefore, the emergence of an alternative path is a direct challenge, since this collaboration between Russia, China and Nicaragua is a powerful geostrategic bomb in his backyard, which will change the history of the region and of the whole world.

This Nicaraguan channel is an emergent strategic opportunity for China, an example of how it is transforming Latin America before the noses of the USA; from its economic structure to its physical infrastructure and even its political dynamics.

In addition, the Canal revenues will be for 100 years for the Chinese business group HKND, and not for Nicaragua.

The Nicaraguan philo-communist government has ceded the country's sovereignty to this concession granted to China, which includes rights for 100 years to exploit, develop and operate not only the Canal, but other projects such as Corinto and Monkey Point (trade hubs), a rail link connecting the Atlantic to the Pacific, and a new international airport.

The largest logistics project in the Western Hemisphere will take place in a country where there is a Castro-Communist regime, aggravated by the location of Nicaragua on the highways of traffic between drug producing countries of the Andean zone to introduce it into USA and Canada.

Due to the high levels of corruption in Nicaraguan institutions, and given the history of narco-trafficking support of the Sandinistas, Nicaragua's new channel would logically attract counter-narcotics, money laundering, and other illicit activities, transforming the zone in a pole of criminality.

More than 30,000 people on the Canal route will be expropriated. The Caribbean of Nicaragua is the nerve center of the peasant movement that opposes the construction of the interoceanic canal.

The indigenous peoples of the Miskito's and Ulwa, as well as the Ramas and Creoles communities, have denounce the Sandinista government in the Inter-American Commission on Human Rights (IACHR).

The people of El Tule and the island of Ometepec in Lake Nicaragua oppose the work, which would leave them without their properties and would affect the main freshwater reserve of the country and Central America.

In addition, in the north of the country, in the border region with Honduras has been developing for some 4 years a strong-armed opposition against the pro-communist regime of Daniel Ortega, which has been described as banditry in order not to attract international attention.

In recent years, this little-noticed story is repeated, from the Argentine businessman Francisco Macri, now president, with Chinese capital factories in Tierra del Fuego and his previous role in the Argentine-Chinese consortium of the Belgrano railway system, to resorts in the Caribbean, built by China, to include Baha Mar in the Bahamas, Punta Perla in the Dominican Republic and Bacholet Bay in Grenada.

There is a certain thing, of consummate the Chinese project of the Channel of Nicaragua will change the strategic environment of all the Latin America.

The Bolivarian Axis

Also, under Havana's design, Venezuela managed to forge alliances in Bolivia, Ecuador and Nicaragua, weakening the strong principles established in the Inter-American Democratic Charter approved by the OAS. Thus, Cuba could organize a greater focus of anti-American resistance in the continent supported by Presidents Rafael Correa, Evo Morales, Daniel Ortega and Nicolás Maduro.

At the same time, radicals such as Evo Morales in Bolivia, Correa in Ecuador and Daniel Ortega in Nicaragua were immediately promoted to join the energy alliance: Venezuela-oil, Bolivia-gas, Ecuador-oil, Iran-oil.

It could be said that in this gear Cuba is located as the logistics center for the illegal transfer of services, finance, oil, weapons, technology; as well as the headquarters of fictitious Russian, Iranian, Venezuelan, and other companies liable to evade international restrictions.

Cuba and Venezuela established the Bolivarian Alternative for the Americas (ALBA), an economic alliance of South America and the Caribbean, as an alternative to the North American NAFTA. At Castro's suggestion, Venezuela bought Argentina's foreign debt by securing the confluence of the Kirchner Buenos-airean dynasty.

For its part, the ALBA, in addition to its objective of hindering the Pan-American project of the Free Trade Area of the Americas (FTAA), has promoted the Regional Compensation Unified System (Sucre), the ALBA Bank, and a penetration platform policy based on energy (Petroamérica) and Petrocaribe operating from Cuba.

The radicalization of communism in Venezuela and the empowerment of the group of the Bolivarian Alliance for America (ALBA) has succeeded in separating the United States from the rest of the continent.

As a culmination of this process, the Community of Latin American and Caribbean States (CELAC) was created, in which communist Cuba was not only recognized but also assumed a leading role since its founding. CELAC includes the entire region, but significantly excludes Canada and the United States.

Under the ALBA, the Cuban-Venezuelan company PetroCaribe, which operates from Havana, assured energy dependence on 18 countries in the Caribbean and Central America, seducing them with very low prices.

In the mid-1990s Castro´s brother and Chávez deployed a campaign with the petro-countries of Latin America, Russia and the Middle East, to increase as much as possible, the world price of oil and as a dark side to dislocate the economies of the United States and Europe. From that moment, the price of the barrel would quadruple.

The influence of Cuba was decisive in the Indian movement that crosses the continent, since many of its pictures came from the radical left. In the case of Bolivia, this was increased when in 1993 Castro visited the country.

The life president, Evo Morales comes from a Cochabamba family growing coca. His political career was supported by the Left and especially by the Communist Party of Bolivia. Supported by the Forum of Sao Paulo, he founded his party, Movement to Socialism, which seeks to reconcile indigenism with Marxism, as is the FARC in Colombia.

After 12 years of dictatorship, he has managed to manipulate the elections to remain indefinitely in power. Under his regime there is no free press or political transparency. TV channels, radio and newspapers have been converted into official media. It is notorious the embezzlement of public funds and assassinates journalists and leaders of the opposition and there are of political prisoners.

In October 2013, The Wall Street Journal noted: "With the opposition cornered, Morales has made Bolivia an international center for organized crime and a haven for terrorists. The US Drug Enforcement Administration (DEA) was expelled. Information from the United Nations shows that cocaine production has been rising in Bolivia since 2006 and there are unconfirmed reports that Mexican, Russian and Colombian delinquents have traveled to the country to try to obtain part of the pie. "

Bolivia's President Evo Morales has facilitated visas for Iranian and Palestinian elements, while declaring Israel a "terrorist state." The visit of former Iranian defense minister Ahmad Vahidi in 2011 was noteworthy to conclude secret military and intelligence deals. Vahidi is reclaimed by Interpol as a terrorist.

Also, in the Bolivian town of Santa Cruz, there is a network of indoctrination of Islamic fundamentalism, and they have an armed, para-military arm, the Plurinational Association of Reservists of Tahuantinsuyo (ASPRET).

The center and ASPRET work closely with the Islamic organization Inkarri Islam to recruit and indoctrinate uprooted youth throughout the country.

All this rise of Islamic fundamentalism in Peru and Bolivia to promote the Iranian revolution in both countries, began to develop from the visit of Fidel Castro to Iran and then to these Latin American countries in 1993.

Through these Islamic centers, Iran and HizbAllah are being introduced into the indigenous population.

Bolivia has negotiated agreements with China for $ 7 trillion. It is also acquiring weapons made in Cuba, as well as training aircraft, ammunition and grenade replacement.

The defense ministers of Russia and Bolivia, Sergey Shoigú and Reymi Ferreira respectively, signed a military cooperation agreement in 2016. Russia agreed to design and construct warships for the armies of Cuba, Nicaragua, Venezuela and Bolivia, and establish licensed production facilities to manufacture Russian-designed military weapons and equipment in these Latin American countries, such as patrol vessels and ships Escorts

Russian President Vladimir Putin has repeatedly pointed out that the European Union (EU) and United States embargo against Moscow has created a good opportunity for Latin American countries to increase their cooperation with Russia.

"We are now working with other producers, Latin American countries, Brazil, Argentina, Chile, and Eastern partner countries like China," Putin said recently, and considered it "ridiculous" for European governments to convince Latin American countries that do not export their products to the Russian market.

Mexico, Central America
and the Caribbean

The region comprising Mexico, Central America and the Caribbean, which in many respects constitute three separate regions, with barely a third of the total population of Latin America, concentrates almost half of the US investment, more than 70% of the Inter-American trade and around 85% of the migration to the US.

By the 1980s, American leaders still considered important "national security" considerations about Grenada, El Salvador and Nicaragua, derived mainly from Castro-communist interference.

But, in the current context, the relationship and attention of the US with the Caribbean Basin and the Southern Cone move in opposite directions, and with the Andean countries they also follow a different path.

In the years before the First World War, the North Americans the political influence of the United States in the Caribbean and Central America was quite large by capital investment and trade, to the point of being considered "the American lake".

Towards the end of the Cold War, although geopolitics and military technologies changed, attention and importance declined to that area, along with that of the Panama Canal.

Washington no longer deploys a single "Latin American policy," but different bilateral or sub-regional strategies: still exercises an even more overwhelming economic and cultural influence for countries located in its border region, not politics. The nature and dynamics of relations with that countries are increasingly different from those of the rest of the region as they form an area deeply mixed through trade and massive migration of unprecedented dimensions in history.

Relations between the US and its close neighbors pose particularly complex challenges due to lack of border control, illegal immigration, drug and arms trafficking, car theft, money laundering, natural disasters, environmental protection, public health, corruption and compliance with the law.

The Mexican drug cartels have extensive links with the government of President Maduro in Venezuela. The drug is transported in Venezuelan military aircraft from Maracaibo to the Sinaloa cartel.

Youth gangs and criminal leaders, many of them socialized in the US and deported to their countries of origin, are wreaking havoc in several Central American nations. On the other hand, the Latin bands are destabilizing factors in the life of Los Angeles and other American cities.

Migrant remittances are vital for many economies. In Mexico, they total more than 30 trillion dollars, almost as much as direct foreign investment. In Central America, Haiti and the Dominican Republic, the amount of remittances exceeds that of foreign investment and international economic assistance added.

Likewise, their economies rely overwhelmingly on American tourism, investment, imports and technology; they absorb popular culture and fashions from and also baseball players for the US leagues.

The Caribbean Basin continues to be a top security area. Because of its proximity and the weight of financial investments within the continent, it has strategic significance in programs of assistance such as the Caribbean Basin Security Initiative (CBSI).

US policy toward the Caribbean Basin should expand bilateral agreements in the energy field as well as in defense and security in SouthCom's medium- and long-term activities with CARICOM and the Dominican Republic; including the Strategy to Combat Illicit Trafficking in the Caribbean (CCITS).

The aim is to dismantle transnational organized crime networks, such as illicit trafficking in drugs, human beings and weapons.

The national disintegration and the violence unleashed since the Revolution of 1910, for the control of drug trafficking in large territories of the Republic, are very important to know the criminal nature of the Mexican State, deeply penetrated by organized crime.

From 1960 to 2000, the government of the PRI (Institutional Revolutionary Party) negotiated with the different drug cartels, assigning them territories, and allowing them to traffic and cross the border into the United States, with the condition that there was no violence and that the drug did not stay in Mexico. The shipments were guarded by the police and military themselves to the border, to make sure that the drug did not stay in Mexico.

It was a pact based on corruption because the different governments of the PRI charged them taxes. By then the government got involved with those criminal groups.

In the 1980s, drug money corrupted important institutions, such as the Attorney General's Office, the Ministry of Defense, and the Federal Judicial Police.

The expansion and success of organized crime in Mexico is the story of a political failure since the Government of Miguel de la Madrid, (1982-1988) who, in 1985, launched the first offensive against drug trafficking in response to the murder of DEA agent Enrique Camarena, at the hands of the Guadalajara Cartel.

The consequent dismantling of the Guadalajara Cartel and the Gulf Cartel led to the emergence of three other cartels: the Sinaloa, Juarez and Tijuana cartels.

During the government of Miguel de la Madrid, his head of Security, José Antonio Zorrilla, ordered the murder of the journalist Manuel Buendía who highlighted the drug trafficking link with the federal authorities and the Army.

At that time, the Secretary of Defense himself, Juan Arevalo Gardoqui, was accused by US federal courts of receiving bribes from drug trafficking.

During the mandate of Carlos Salinas (1988-1994), the tentacles of drug trafficking reached the presidential family, implicating the brother of the president.

The Tijuana Cartel, of the Arellano Félix, grew under the shadow of the Salinas and Ernesto Zedillo governments (1994-2000), while the Juarez Cartel would reach immense power under the guidance of Amado Carrillo Fuentes, "the Lord of the heavens".

President Zedillo was also involved in drug trafficking scandals, especially with the Juarez Cartel. In addition, during his presidency, General Jesús Gutiérrez Rebollo, his anti-drug czar, and his National Defense Secretary, Enrique Cervantes Aguirre were linked to the same Cartel.

These groups began to grow protected by the governments of the PRI, and when it was thought, in the year 2000, that a transitional government began, nothing changed, except, the pretension to monopolize the activities of the Sinaloa cartel.

The problem of drug trafficking deepens when Vicente Fox arrives at the presidency of Mexico in 2000. General Anabel Hernández has denounced the links of the Mexican government with drug trafficking. According to him, the Sinaloa cartel had paid more than 20 million dollars to President Vicente Fox to free the cartel chief, Chapo Guzmán.

After leaving the prison, the government begins a police and military battle against the enemy drug trafficking groups of the Sinaloa cartel, to create a drug monopoly where a single cartel controls the entire market.

The government of President Felipe Calderón (Mexico 2006-2012), also had direct contacts with Chapo Guzmán who has ratified it.

When the current Mexican president, Enrique Peña Nieto, belonging to the PRI, came to power in 2012, he imposed a halt to the frontal strategy of the "war on drugs" that the previous president of Calderón had established, alleging that it would reduce the levels of violence.

The government of was plagued with corruption scandals. The Brazilian construction company Odebrecht involved the president Peña Nieto, who received $ 1.5 million in 2012 from the company for his presidential campaign, through Braskem, a petrochemical subsidiary.

The main fault that the last three presidents have committed -Fox, Calderón and Peña Nieto- is that they have lacked strategy and overall vision, showing their incapacity and not institutional leadership to add the three powers: executive, legislative and judicial.

The weakness of the State, the corruption of the authorities, the failure of the Rule of Law and the lack of a comprehensive drug policy are the ingredients of the recipe for the expansion of drug trafficking and the consequent increase in violence. The different governments of Mexico have not exercised all their authority to fight drug trafficking, because in their turns they have taken sides with one of the cartels.

With the consent of political, governmental, police and military power, a violent war of cartels was built that has spread to other countries. Mexico reached 19,000 homicides at the end of 2016, a figure that represents an increase of 3.2% over the previous year. The number of kidnappings and extortions has also increased.

The worsening of the clashes between drug trafficking groups in Mexican territory puts the United States on alert to achieve greater control in the area, thus avoiding risks to the northern society. The US Congress has calculated that between 19 and 29 billion dollars of illicit profits go to the drug trafficking cartels.

The extensive border that divides both countries, with the surveillance difficulties that it represents, is a propitious way for the passage of drug trafficking and also for terrorism.

Brazil

Analyzing foreign policy in Latin America is always a challenge. Different geographies, different actors, different links with the international system, give rise to very dissimilar foreign policies.

The United States must regain momentum in the inter-American relations, halt the advance of extra-regional powers (mainly China and Russia) and limit the aspirations of Mercosur or Unasur. That is why the Pacific Alliance is fundamental to attract dissenting Mercosur countries like Uruguay and Paraguay.

The readjustment of state powers in Western Europe before the crisis of the European Union; the repositioning of the emerging powers grouped in the BRICS bloc and in the conformation of new leaderships in the G20, influences the new role of Brazil as a global player, given the demand for greater symmetry within the Latin American region, a premise defended by the South-Latin American integration blocks.

Brazil, the sixth largest economy in the world and increasingly a global player as part of the BRICS, and also in the region remains the largest backward of the cold war, the US blockade of Cuba

The Mercosur countries, of which Brazil is the most extensive, account for 45% of the population, almost 60% of Latin American GDP, more than 40% (in increasing proportion) of US investment and much less than 10% of migration Latin American to the USA.

Extensive negotiations with Mercosur should be undertaken to prevent them from adopting agreements that hamper compliance with the strategic and general objectives of the hemispheric projection of the United States.

In the "hemispheric security" strategy, in addition to joint military exercises, mention should be made of Plan Colombia, the "Andean Regional Initiative", the Mérida Plan, and the Southern Command.

During the presidencies of Reagan and Bush, Brazil aspired to a "special relationship" with the USA, mainly because both administrations understood that the South American giant could not be dispensed with.

Despite its immense problems and challenges, Brazil is an increasingly successful and influential country, which occupies an important place in international trade and in environmental negotiations, public health and intellectual property.

It has opened its economy to international competition; is an active and influential leader in the global South, and works closely with India and South Africa.

The criterion was (now lost) that cooperation between the two countries was and is not only an economic, political or diplomatic necessity, but above all a geographic fact. The map of the hemisphere shows the enormous size of these two territorial masses, with large population groups and who need to maintain close ties, above divergences.

Time ago, Arthur Schlesinger Jr. had pointed out that, just as the future of democracy in Asia depends heavily on the example of India, the future of democracy in Latin America depends considerably on the example of Brazil.

In the last decades (from Presidents Clinton to Obama) Brazil has abandoned its "traditional friendship" with the United States. Its alliance with the USA reflected an economic complementarity in which Brazil's sales depended on exports, in equal proportion, of the North American market.

So, Brazil embarked on consolidating its zone of influence in South America, through organizations such as the Union of South American Nations (UNASUR) and the Community of Latin American and Caribbean States (CELAC), seeking to become together with Cuba as the arbiter of regional tensions.

Actually, Brazil is committed to making the leap to the global stage as a relevant actor, and believes that USA is the main obstacle to achieve its goal.

Brazil has one of the 10 largest industrial parks in the world, diversified in its exports of manufactures and advanced technology products, which supplanted sugar, coffee and cocoa.

In 2009 Brazil stimulated opposition throughout South America to block the USA military bases in Colombia; and expressed its opposition to the USA position regarding the events of Honduras.

Today, Brazil disagrees in many political aspects with the USA, and has become the leader of the region, capitalizing on the void left by the USA and the inability of the Obama administration to decipher Latin America.

The perception of two Americas is the current objective of Brazil's foreign policy, which seeks to establish its hegemony in Mexico, Central America and the Caribbean, thus dividing the Western Hemisphere into two parts: the North (USA and Canada) "North American", and the "Brazilian" South. For this, the key is Cuba.

The long-term project conceived by Brazil is to use the influence of communist Cuba as a basis for its policy towards Central America and the Caribbean, and in the future as a bridge to access the USA market.

One of the most discrepant aspects is precisely Cuba, since it supports the participation of Havana in all matters of the hemisphere, through its adhesion to the Rio Group, to the point of granting subsidized financial loans.

Brazil bitterly criticized the United States for not supporting its request for a permanent bank in the United Nations Security Council and voting for India.

The administrations of Lula da Silva and Dilma Rousseff (the left wing of the Workers' Party, PT) have prioritized relations with Venezuela, Argentina, and other countries with leftist governments, and have not sought to improve ties with Washington.

It also showed his disagreement over relations with Paraguay after the impeachment against President Fernando Lugo; its rejection of the US military bases in Colombia; on the role of the Organization of American States and its Inter-American Commission on Human Rights.

Brazil also defends the Iranian nuclear arms program and has opposed United Nations sanctions against Tehran, supporting the Iranian president's nine Latin American tours, and has become Iran's main trading partner in Latin America. At the same time, it maintains a pro-Palestinian position in the Arab-Israeli conflict.

The Mercosur issue became the main rivalry between Brazil and the USA, because it involved deep contradictions and intertwining of economic, political and strategic interests. Henry Kissinger considered that Mercosur was intended to be something like the EU, not only as a political identity distinct from the United States but a clear opposition.

The negotiations on world trade are a point of friction between the two countries, and Brazil has been inclined to France in the international arena, specifying military agreements. Brazil defended multilateral solutions in response to 9/11 and rejected the FTAA; to tariffs on Brazilian ethanol; advocates in the Doha Round that the USA reduce agricultural subsidies.

With Brazil, political dialogue, including aspects of military cooperation and security issues, should be sponsored and bilateral initiatives in economic, scientific and educational fields proliferated.

The Southern Cone
and the Andean zone

The Andean zone must constitute a focus of greater North American concern, due to political instability and drug trafficking. These countries located outside the immediate geographical area, that is, the large states of South America (Argentina, Brazil and Chile) may try to neutralize the North American influence through common action or through the use of powers from outside the Hemisphere, because today they have a margin of maneuver that did not exist in the past.

The countries of the Southern Cone represent less than 40% of US investment, only 15% of interregional trade, and contribute only about 10% of migrants to North America. Today, the priorities of this sub-region are increasingly in China its main market and partner; it has been a sub-region historically with a distant relationship with North America.

The Southern Cone seeks a commercial opening, opening and with a geographical location towards the Pacific, unlike the Caribbean environment. This is the Pacific Alliance, which has its origin in the Latin American Pacific Arc, which varies according to its location in the hierarchy of regional power.

These countries are close to the United States, have free trade agreements that have seen in the

Alliance a means to rearrange themselves in Latin America and counterbalance other regional groups and countries such as Cuba and Venezuela.

The geo-strategic importance of the Pacific Alliance lies in its capabilities and positioning in the hierarchy of regional power and the possibility of being a bridge of Latin America with the Asia-Pacific. The characteristics of its members and the weakening of countries that exercised regional leadership such as Brazil and Venezuela, contribute in this regard.

All Andean countries, to varying degrees, are plagued by severe governance problems and have weak political institutions. To this must be added the unresolved integration of large indigenous populations that are increasingly heard, and of the many -not only indigenous- who live in poverty or indigence.

Peru's economy depends on exports of fishmeal and fish oil. For its part, Mexico for several years, has paid great attention to its Pacific region, rich in flora and fauna. The Colombian Pacific presents security problems, poor infrastructure and low development, with the region being hit hardest by armed groups and violence. It has a single deep port, and very precarious communication channels.

In these circumstances, Washington must emphasize and strengthen much more a growing awareness in a democratic market economy context, to cooperate in the eradication of flagrant economic inequality, widespread poverty.

The US must focus new attention on the construction of adequate concepts, policies and institutions to improve its particular interdependence with South America, which must also address comparable efforts to rethink and redesign regional approaches, international connections and relations, both with Washington and with other centers of world power.

Argentina and Chile

Unlike Brazil, for example, that has a foreign policy marked by continuity, likewise Chile and Colombia, historically, Argentina is characterized by fluctuations, which fails to define a coherent foreign policy agenda. Domestic, ever-changing considerations have always determined its position.

Argentina has had great difficulties in building consensus, strengthening institutions, opening up its entire economy and achieving the predictability that is so important to facilitate sustainable development.

Although the country has actively participated in international affairs and has been an ally of the United States in the fight against terrorism and drug trafficking and in the non-proliferation of nuclear weapons, it is much less important from the American point of view than its pompous designation as "extra-NATO ally" might suggest.

There is a negative notion that he cannot count on significant empathy or concrete US support, no matter who rules in Washington. It is possible that US support for England in the Falklands war and the failure of the Bush administration to rescue Argentina during its deep economic crisis of 2001-2002 have influenced this suspicion towards Washington.

It is true that Argentina has occupied a place of low strategic relevance for the interests of

Washington and, as in the case of other South American countries, the economic dimension of the link is, for the moment, the most complex. Therefore, it has been refractory to accepting a greater economic, political and military presence of Washington in the Southern Cone.

The United States left Argentina to its fate during the crisis of 2001, and from that moment, the relation between Buenos Aires and Washington has been marked by the distance.

In financial and economic terms, the bilateral relationship was "difficult" due to Argentina's failure to comply with the international financial community

Beginning with the problems of the argentines bonds in the court of New York. It is necessary for Argentina to regularize its links with the international financial community, and in that the USA can influence favorably in such normalization.

The country aims to realize its own energy revolution, and USA has the technology and capital to reproduce oil development, but so far there has been no agreement in that field.

For example, the new government in Argentina might be more receptive to increasing its cooperation with the United States, much more than it has been since the beginning of the century.

President Mauricio Macri's current Argentina is more interested in defining a foreign policy, unlike previous administrations, seeking a model of economic openness and re-establishment of relations with the world, and a more moderate stance towards Washington and inter-American agencies.

President Macri has shown his commitment to strengthen relations with the United States under the criterion that economic reforms should transform Argentina into a main driver of growth in the Western Hemisphere.

There are about 500 US companies in the country. There are also bilateral agreements that can be deepened, such as the Framework for Trade and Investment, which recognizes the fundamental role of trade and private investment in further developing growth and job creation.

There is also the telecommunications field, which includes consultations with the Federal Communications Commission regarding spectrum management and regulatory reform.

Argentina has a strong and dynamic atomic sector for energy and medical use. And, it is key to the fight against the networks of international terrorism and the flows of drug trafficking

In other areas where the bilateral relationship can be expanded: interchange in universities and technical schools, software development, peaceful use of Antarctica, alternative and non-polluting energies, development of the production of shale-gas and shale-oil, the second and fourth world reserves respectively.

Regarding the election of President Macri, USA Senator Marco Rubio has affirmed that after years of corruption, impunity and serious errors of economic management, "the last presidential election of Argentina has given that Nation and USA a new opportunity to revive Our bilateral relationship. "

Senator Kaine has also said that it is important that the new administration, with Donald Trump as USA president, continue to strengthen economic and defense ties with Argentina, because it is an important ally not a member of NATO.

Chile, for its part, is the Latin American country most committed to the world economy; it has the relatively stable institutions and the most established democratic norms and practices in the region. It does not face serious problems of indigenous integration, today it is as linked to the economies of Asia, Europe and Latin America as it is to the North American one.

In turn, Chile has an external policy closely linked to economic-commercial promotion.

Chile, with an extension on the Pacific much higher than that of other Andean countries has built a broad consensus around many key public policies, with a high degree of predictability that facilitates investment, both national and foreign, and promotes strategic planning government and the private sector.

The international influence of Chile and its priority for the US are considerably greater than its dimensions, its military power or its economic weight could suggest. His "soft power" attracts attention and investment and is the key to his leadership and influence.

The Colophon

In the first decades after World War II, the USA developed a successful policy towards the American continent. It succeeded in strengthening the inter-American system in 1947, with the Inter-American Treaty of Reciprocal Assistance (TIAR) and, a year later, it formed the Organization of American States (OAS).

Also, many Latin American nations contributed with troops in the Korean War, especially Colombia, Cuba and Puerto Rico.

In 1961, the Alliance for Progress was launched, a program of economic, political and social development promoted by the USA that until its abrupt and lamentable completion in 1970 would inject $ 20 billion

After the collapse of the communist world, important Latin American countries called for a new approach between the two Americas, an opportunity that was not taken advantage of by the administrations of the day.

In 1990, President George Bush launched the Initiative for the Americas. President "Bill" Clinton would finalize the Initiative for the Americas project, with the first Inter-American Summit of Heads of State. Within the framework of the Washington Consensus, the United States promoted the Free Trade Area of the Americas

(FTAA) and, to implement this hegemonic project, proposed to hold presidential summits.

As the then Secretary of State Colin Powell frankly put it, "our goal with the FTAA is to guarantee US companies control of territory from the Arctic Pole to Antarctica, and free access, without any obstacles or Difficulty for our products, services, technology and capital throughout the hemisphere "

In this sense, the strategy developed towards Latin America and the Caribbean, added to the effects of European colonialism and imperialism, has historically been a key and often determining factor in the development of the nations that belong to this geographical region,

But in recent decades, Latin American policy in the United States has been conceived more as a sum of bilateral or sub-regional military and security treatments than a coherent, globally harmonious design.

The OAS, for example, has become a dysfunctional organization, especially when it comes to addressing the challenges of the region.

While the United States remains a particularly important trading partner for Mexico, Central America and the Caribbean, its trade with the region has been declining, with imports from Latin America and the Caribbean decreasing from 60% to 39%.

The capacity for power exercised by the USA (economic, military, political-diplomatic, ideological, technological) must decisively influence the internal and external policies of the countries of the region.

In addition, the USA exerts a large financial impact, not only because it is the main foreign investor and market for goods and services, the dollar makes up the majority of monetary reserves and because of its influence on exchange rates, because they coexist including total or partially dollarized economies.

The possibility of greater cooperation between Latin American and Caribbean nations is inextricably linked to American action; it is a challenging and difficult process, in which it is fundamental for these countries to reach the knowledge of the North American strategy, seeking to understand it in all its complexity.

An investment policy of the US bank is important to allow less complex access to markets, raw materials and labor, and the penetration of Russia and China is limited, protecting the US markets.

The USA must promote in Latin America the construction of a modern and integrated industrial system coupled with the reconstruction of the rural sector, as well as the consolidation of social progress and the creation of an authentic democracy.

As happened around the market economy in Peru and Chile, during the decade 1980 that helped establish the pillars for the economic reform programs in the following decade. Chile thus became an example of "shock therapy", under the supervision of the so-called Chicago

Boys, influenced by Milton Friedman's monetarist policies.

With respect to massive illegal immigration from Mexico and Central América, because they maintain their ethnic-cultural character, they can affect the identity in the country of destination.

If Venezuela-Castro communist continue to influence the region its policies will negatively impact the global interests of the USA. It is necessary to influence continental energy policy, and to monitor the breadth and depth of relations with Cuba, Russia, China and Iran.

BIBLIOGRAPHY

Benemelis, Juan F. *The Wars of Saddam*. GAD. Miami, 2003.

-Cuba: *Assessing the Threat to US Security*. November 2001. CANF. 143 p.

-*The end of a Utopia*. Benya Publishers, Miami 2005. 500 p.

-*Soviet Bloc Transition*. Fundación CubaFuturo, US, 2006. 900 p.

-*The Red Dragon: China*. Benya Publishers, Miami, 2007, 332 p.

-*XX Century Geo-Politic*. Benya Publishers, Miami, 2009, 296 p.

-*The Koran and the Prophet*. ZC Editor, Miami, 2009, 542 p.

-*Islam and Terrorism*. ZC Ed., Miami. 2010, 190 p.

-*The New Century*. The Ceiba Institute, Miami, 2012, 428 p.

-*The Roots of Terrorism*. The Ceiba Institute, US, 2013, 412 p.

-*The Bolsheviks*. The Ceiba Institute, Miami, 2012, 430 p

-*Islam Civilization & politics*. Benya Publishers, US 2015. 256 p.

Cohen, Ariel. *Russian Imperialism, development and crisis*. Westport, Conn.: Praeger Publishers, 1996.

Davis, Philip. *Bernard Malamud: A Writer's Life*. (2007)

Fiori, Jose Luis. (November 24, 2007). Nicholas Spykman e to Latin America. Le Monde Diplomatique.

Glennon, Michael J. Why the Security Council Failed. In *Foreign Affairs*. May/June 2003, p. 23.

Goldman, Marshall I. *What Went Wrong with Perestroika?* W.W. Norton Company. N Y, 1991: 173.

Gorbachov, Mikhail. *Perestroika: mi mensaje a Rusia y al mundo entero.* Ediciones B, S. A. Barcelona, 1987: 185.

Harris, Nigel. *The end of the Third World*. London, Harmondsworth - Penguin 1987, pp. 102-103.

Henry Holt. Resource Wars: *The New Landscape of Global Conflict*. Metropolitan, 2001.

Jaramillo Edwards, Isabel. The strategic political dimensions: The United States and the cases of Mexico, Colombia and Venezuela. CNA, 2003-2004, p. 58

Kennan, George F. (1951), *American Diplomacy, 1900–1950*, Chicago: University of Chicago Press, OCLX.

Mahan, Alfred Thayer. (1890) The influence of sea power upon history Boston: Little, Brown and Company's.

Marglin Stephen, Judith B. Schor. *The Goleen Age of Capitalism: Reinterpreting the Post-War Experience*. Oxford, Clarendon Press, 1990.

Murphy Richard, "Out of Sight: What is a Tax Haven" April 4th 2011 http://www.lrb.co .uk / v33 / n08 /.

News, Mexico, April 27, 2001, p. a4.

O`Donnell Guillermo, and Schmitier, Philippe. *Transitions from Authoritarian Rule: Tentative Conclusions about Uncertain Democracies.* Baltimore: Johns Hopkins Univ., Press. 1994: 19.

Pfaff, William. *Lonely New World.* Feb. 28, 2000.

Peak Oil. 24 November 05.

Polanyi, Karl. *The Great Transformation.* New York: Farrar and Reinhart, 1994, pp. 50-51.

Riordan Roett poses as a matter of national security. Foreign relations of Mexico in the decade of the nineties. Mexico. 21st century, 1991, pp. 86-101.

Rochester, Stuart and Frederick Riley's book *Honor Bound. American Prisoners of War in Southeast Asia, 1961-1973.* Naval Institute Press (January 15, 2013).

Rosales, Osvaldo. Mikio Kuwayama. Economic Commission for Latin America and the Caribbean (ECLAC). Santiago, April 2012.

Soberón, Ricardo. Drug trafficking trends in Latin America. At: www.tni.org. 1997.

Suchlicki, Jaime. Director of the Institute for Cuban and Cuban-American Studies. Miami, September 2001.

Walker, Tony. *World Bank Urges China to Privatize.* Financial Times, 18 de Julio: 7, 1997.

Wolf, Markus and Anne McElvoy. *Man, without a Face. The Autobiography of Communism's Greatest Spymaster.* NY, 1997: Ch. 9.

Zakaria, Fareed. *The Future of Freedom,* NY: W. W. Norton, 2003.